BEHIND ENEMY LINES

The Autobiography of

NICHOL COLLINS

BEHIND ENEMY LINES

Cover designed by Professional Identity Partners
myprofessionalidentity.com

ISBN- 978-0-9997545-1-1

Printed in the United States of America.

Color photos are inserted throughout different chapters.

Names have been changed to protect the innocent.

chosen2witness.com

Table of Contents

Forewords

The uniqueness of J. Nichol Collins' book is not the experiences she relates, but the power contained within its pages. Her genuine repentance, and complete surrender to the Holy Ghost unleashes the spiritual tools necessary to effectively minister deliverance to all that are bound in perversion and sin. As her mother, I witnessed this breathtaking metamorphosis transformation. The incidents occurring in her autobiography are unbelievably true. God moved me 2,000 miles away so He could deal with Nichol personally. After years of prayer, the Lord snatched her from the enemy's camp. I was not going to allow Satan to destroy my seed. I commanded the Devil to Let My Baby Go! I was confident of this one thing, He that had begun a good work in her would perform it until the day of Jesus Christ. This book is not just for readers struggling with their sexual identity, but brings awareness to so many subjects.

-Evangelist Yevette Fisher

Author of Devil Let My Baby Go

In her autobiography, Behind Enemy Lines, Evangelist Nichol Collins has penned an effective weapon for the use of the church by exposing the demonic ploys of the most prevalent perversion sweeping the world today. In every generation, there arises a chosen vessel who dares to cross the boundaries of convention that embody the man-made customs, traditions, and beliefs considered politically correct. Nichol Collins is one of these exceptional few world changers and Kingdom builders.

-Evangelist Karolyn Chaney

Author of Minding Things

Nichol Collins has a testimony that will literally blow your mind. God has delivered her from bondage, and now she has an incredible opportunity to help others be delivered. Her passion for Christ jumps off the pages of this book. Homosexuality is a taboo subject in many churches. I'm so thankful she has the strength to share her amazing testimony that others can also experience God's saving grace and soon return.

-Presiding Bishop Eric Lloyd

Rhema Int'l Fellowship of Churches

The seed of transformation is activated by a declared and predestined set time. Through persecution, life's pain, and an undesirable journey Nichol is more than a conqueror. Evangelist Collins was birthed, tried by the fire, chosen of God and TRANSFORMED through the beauty of HOLINESS. She is a re-created vessel of honor with a proven word of testimony

-Pastor J. Alexander Morris

Pentecostal Assemblies of the World

Nichol Apostolic is a voice of deliverance for this generation. Her candid straight forward approach will cause you to see the depths of sin she had fallen into. More importantly, the saving grace of Jesus Christ plucked her out of the hand of the enemy. I count it a privilege to call this awesome woman of God a co-laborer in the gospel of Jesus Christ. You will discover that through her no holds barred story Behind Enemy Lines, Nichol is a force to be reckoned with.

-Pastor Gregory N. Winley

Balanced Believers Ministries

Dedication

This book is dedicated to my late Grandmother's, Lera Fisher and Ethel Lee Wyatt. You both were full of love. I know you would be Godly proud of me today. I am a product of your prayers on my behalf.

Mom, I have no idea what my fate, or state of mind would have been if you had not stuck 'Behind Enemy Lines' with me. You have been a real trooper marching in the 'Army of the Lord.' Mom you remained steadfast, unmovable, always abounding in the work of the Lord. I expressed to you on many occasions that you did not fail as a parent causing me to become gay. I made a choice to live my life in chaos. I am appreciative that you used a strategy of warfare to combat against the devil's agenda to kill me. I came out with NO RESIDUE! I thank you for making me conscious in my Caterpillar stages about breaking habits of learned behavior. I am glad you lived to see my DELIVERANCE. I love you to life!

Dad, thank you for being my father. You have been supportive throughout a lifetime. You have been my hero, always coming to rescue. Love you!

My childhood Pastor/Bishop, you instilled the Apostles doctrine in me. You trained up a child in the way that they should go, and I have not departed from the Acts 2:38 "Tenements of the Faith." Thank you for living as a holy example. Your late wife was truly like another Mother. I was blessed to be mentored by her. Shalom!

Auntie Ivy, I thank God for you laboring with me at the altar to receive the Holy Ghost. You have been a supportive instrument of counsel through the years. I recall you warning me not to get entangled in homosexuality, but I didn't take heed. I am glad to be back in fellowship. I love you dearly!

Aunt Lona, thanks to you, Deacon Hendrick, "the prayer warrior" Aunt Renee, Dayna, Devin, and Darren for being family to us. You have opened your home on several occasions. I appreciate the generosity and support from your family. Much love to y'all!

Uncle Dwight and Auntie Denise, I am so grateful for you allowing me to stay at your house during my transition out of the lifestyle. Hiding out at your house kept me alive. Thank You! Love you guys.

A big thank you to Aunt "K", Evangelist Chaney who spent countless hours making sure this book was birthed in a spirit of excellence. I appreciate you for your prayers throughout the years. Love you dearly!

A sincere thank you to all those who travailed in prayer concerning me.

My Arrival

The devil tried to kill me before I was even born. One day my mom who was pregnant with me at the time was in a car accident. I was displaced out of the birthing position. She was rushed to the hospital. On Thanksgiving Day, November 22nd, after my mom was in labor for 22 hours, I finally arrived. I was born to Compton's notorious childhood sweethearts Yevette Fisher and Edward Collins. Everyone knew my dad by his nickname "Skip." All their friends and families were anxious to lay eyes on me. Jeremiah 1:5 (NLT) says, *"I knew you before I formed you in your mother's womb. Before you were born I set you apart as my prophet to the nations."*

My Grandma Lera conveyed to me years later that moments after I entered the world, I looked up at them as if I had been here before. She had given birth to eleven children, and described how I was not wrinkled up or frowning like they were. Grandma said the expression on my face was funny. 'What are you Negroes looking at?' is what they imagined me saying.

My mom fled from my dad Skip's physical abuse when I was a two-month old infant. She decided it was not safe to live in that type of environment. As intelligent as my father was, he sold drugs for a living. His actions had become outlandish experimenting with sherm, which is a cigarette dipped in embalming fluid. As I grew older, I gained knowledge of his violent past toward my mother. Besides being smart, it sounds like he was psychotically obsessive. The stories reminded me of the movie "What's Love Got to Do with It."

As a single parent, my mom sought career-based employment. She was hired at a travel reservations center. Right away, she met a slightly older man on her job named Jack Rivers. It seems as if she did not allow herself the time to heal after her break up with my father. Humanity itself lives by the slogan, "on to the next one." Jack was a married man with two children by his wife. At first, as a solution to keep my stalking abusive father Skip away from her, my mom entertained the attention from Jack.

They began dating when I was four months old. My mom tried to send Jack back to his wife twice. However, her rejection motivated him to pursue her persistently. He was very romantic while splurging significant amounts of money on dates. Eventually, he grew on her, and they got an apartment together in Cyprus, Ca.

On two separate occasions, my biological father shot through the apartment window and busted out Jack's car windows. What an irrational decision my father made with me inside the house. It is true, there is a thin line between love and hate. He was not letting my mother move on with her life easily.

I inherited my ingenious traits from my dad's side of the family. I was told by my relatives that I was an extraordinary child. As a baby, I got teeth early, started walking at seven months, and my speech pronunciation was never baby talk. My mom describes it as if one day, I blurted out perfect English. People thought I could read at two years old because I had memorized Dr. Seuss books. I would sit in the lobby at the doctor's office flipping the pages and reciting words from stories. My mom refused to listen to my Grandma Lera's suggestion to have my IQ level tested. She assumed people would use me as a science experiment if she allowed me to be observed.

New City

We moved to Pasadena, California, Jack's hometown. Compared to the inner city, that was a smaller town to raise children. Our house was a two-level older Victorian-style home with hardwood floors. On the bottom-level there was a huge den, dining room, living room, and kitchen. My parents' room was the only bedroom downstairs. The additional three bedrooms were upstairs.

From the time I was four months, Jack raised me as his own. I called him Dad – never by his first name. He even offered to give me his last name legally, but I did not think it was necessary in order to feel apart of our blended family. Grandma Wyatt, Skip's mother, asked me to keep his last name of Collins.

On Saturdays, I remember spending a lot of time alone watching cartoons. My parents were locked up in their room all the time when they were not working. I could hear moaning as I passed their bedroom to get to the kitchen. Although he was good to me, I often felt like Jack was stealing a lot of Mom's time from me. I suffered from abandonment and sought attention at school being the class clown, super talkative, and an over achiever.

Growing up, I was a very athletic tomboy. My dad Jack was my coach on an all-boys baseball team. I was the only girl in the league at that time. I played three positions: the hardball pitcher, shortstop, and second baseman. I was the center (hiker) on the Pop Warner football team, wearing a helmet and shoulder pads. I played small forward on the co-ed basketball team at the boy's club. Surprisingly, I never suffered any injuries from these sporting activities. My mom missed several of my games because she would be working. Whereas, I appreciated my dad Jack's support, it did not have the same impact as if my mother was there.

As my mother's only child, she spoiled me with material things. I practically got what I wanted as a reward for good grades. We frequented amusement parks, movies, ice skating, and picnics. I loved the Strawberry Shortcake cartoon bike she bought me one Christmas. It was pink with chrome wheels, a banana shaped seat with strawberries on it, and red streamers hanging out of the red handlebar grips. I started off riding on training wheels, then my Uncle Norbert taught me how to balance without them. Unfortunately, I carelessly left my bike in the neighbor's driveway, and he backed over it. What a disappointment it was to see my Strawberry Shortcake as flat as a pancake.

As a kid, my mom wanted me to be girlie. She would make me wear dresses to elementary school every Monday. I despised that because I liked to play during recess, and I felt so inhibited. She put me in ruffled dresses up to my neck with matching socks. I was like her real-life Barbie doll. I was athletic, but I did not mind wearing girls' clothes. Nevertheless, being forced to wear dresses to school was irritating, to me dresses were church apparel.

One year, Mom signed me up for the drill team called the "Soul Patrol." The rehearsals were held at the park at least three times a week. It seemed as if I walked a mile to get there. I would be exhausted after practice walking back home. We marched in a parade for Martin Luther King Day and I cried from start until the finish. Mom was so excited, she jogged beside us taking pictures, and cheering me on. I was thirsty, my feet were hurting, and I had no rhythm. I could not catch on to all that marching, choreography, and hand formation.

Bitter Memories

I remember going to my grandmother's house in Compton on the weekends to visit my biological father, Skip. My aunts and uncles showed me lots of love. I was their only niece and grandchild, so I was always the center of attention over there. My grandmother nicknamed me "Precious." Bonding with my father's side of the family was enjoyable.

Honestly, all I ever felt was love from my father because he treated me like his prized possession. My Aunt Joyce would comb my hair real neat and pretty. I loved taking baths and either my grandma or my Aunt Joyce would wash my back. They would squeeze the washcloth to rinse the soap off as warm water ran down my spine. Afterward, they would dress me up for my father to take me with him. We would first stop at the store, to buy my favorite snacks – Funyuns, and Blue Diamond smoked almonds. Then we would ride around the city of Compton visiting relatives and friends.

One weekend I went to visit my dad Skip. Instead of him taking me to the store, my favorite Uncle Curtis drove me. When we returned we stood in the front yard as I ate my snacks.

"I got some bad news," he said, as he dropped his head sadly, "Your dad died."

"He did?" I asked, looking puzzled.

"Yes niece, he was shot last night," he said, as his voice trembled.

"I hope they get the bad guy," I replied, in a sad tone.

As a six-year-old, I understood exactly what he meant. I was devastated thinking how I would never see my dad again. I was lost for words as my uncle hugged me. It was a heartbreaking tragedy and the worst day imaginable. I was so shocked that I did not cry.

My biological father was murdered two doors from my grandmother's house. He died because a drug deal went sour. The neighbor who shot him was paranoid on drugs. He accused my father of trying to beat him out of money. Some crack went missing in a house full of people. My dad Skip was showing him how to cook cocaine into a rock form. He shot my dad in the head like a cold-hearted killer. The witnesses fled the scene out of fear.

Ultimately, prosecutors never had enough evidence. My dad's killer never spent a day in jail for this brutal murder. CSI (crime scene investigation) was not so advanced. The police department was corrupt and being investigated that year. It appeared as if the killer was under arrest as he was hauled away in handcuffs. However, a neighborhood resident witnessed him being let out the car around the corner.

I remember my father's funeral like it was yesterday. When I viewed his body, he looked asleep, but I knew better. His lips were even sealed closed with a clear substance that resembled saliva. My Aunt Joyce took his death really hard; she was emotionally drunk off a six pack of beer on an empty stomach. She looked at him in the casket, erupted into tears, and vomited all over her dress as she walked out of the service. The reality of her best friend and brother never coming back overwhelmed her.

It was Easter weekend and with all the preparation for the funeral, everyone forgot to buy me an Easter basket, but it didn't matter much. It was a sad day for me – I would never see my father again. I was crushed because I could not understand why he was shot, and no details were given to me then. Moreover, I felt angry that his killer was not being punished. In my little mind, I thought bad guys were supposed to go to jail like what I saw on the cops and robbers' television show.

After my father's death, Grandma Wyatt would rub my hands pulling on my fingers.
"You know, Skip had hands like yours with all these lines in his palms," Grandma said.

"Really Grandma? No, I didn't know that about him," I replied.

She emphasized how much I resembled my father and stared at me a lot. Every time I visited, she loved to talk to me about my father.

She always asked, "Do you remember your father?"

"Yes Grandma, I do very well," I said.

She showed me several pictures to keep my memory of him alive.

It never bothered me that Grandma Wyatt called me 'Precious.' I knew that meant I was special to her. She was a beautiful, dark chocolate colored woman and real classy. She wore designer reading glasses, always drove a new Cadillac, and got her hair and nails done weekly. Grandma Wyatt played bingo and seemed to get lucky often, so she always bought me clothes and tennis shoes. Her profession was an administrator at the Compton Unified School board.

My Grandma Lera was my mom's mother. We rotated spending weekends at her house in Watts, Ca. My uncle Ricky owned a trucking company, so he was able to purchase a big house for her. Since my mom had ten siblings, I had a lot of cousins who came over on weekends to Grandma's. Grandma Lera was a pretty woman, caramel complexion, always dyed her hair honey blonde, and wore fancy hats to church. She loved the Lord and showered us with so much love. She grew fresh vegetables in her garden in the backyard and her greens that she cooked were my favorite. She had so many grandchildren, we ate lots of bologna and grilled cheese sandwiches. The government cheese used to be a huge rectangular-shaped log that seemed to never run out.

I will never forget the weekend I spent at Grandma Lera's house. My Aunt Von had kidnapped her own children from Seattle, Washington. She was in a custody battle with their father. I hid in a small closet under the staircase with my two cousins, but the officer found us and took them. That was the last time I ever saw my cousins.

MY PARENTS

Grandparents (top) Lera & Price Fisher   William & Ethel Wyatt

Nichol Collins

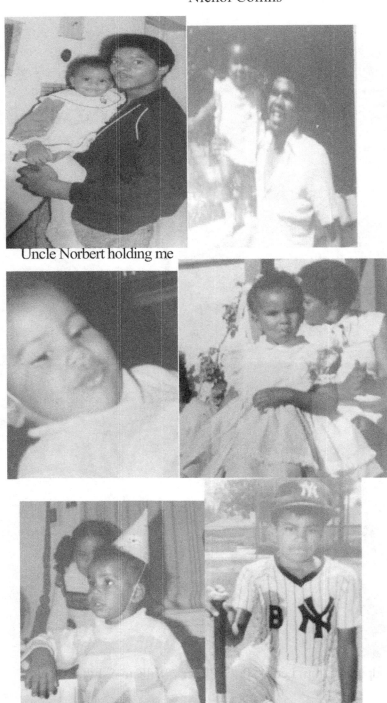

Uncle Norbert holding me

Confused & Abused

After six years of living together, Mom and Jack decided to get married. I referred to Jack as my Dad now that my father Skip was deceased. My parents were constantly assisting family members in the time of need. I had a cousin named Carl who was more like a brother to me. His mother had some challenges so she sent him to reside with (us) his Uncle Jack. My uncles on my mother's side stayed for short periods of time while enduring hardships. Having had eight brothers and two sisters, it was always likely that Mom would have to help someone facing a dilemma.

Our family was dysfunctional. My dad smoked marijuana from the time I could remember. He was kind to me, but on occasion he was grumpy when he ran out of marijuana. He had a porn addiction, and a couple of times left movies in my VCR by accident. The video cassette recorder in my parents' room was broken, so he would watch porn in my bedroom while I was at school.

It was depressing the way my dad was verbally abusive causing my mom to cry. I recall my mother and I taking long rides as tears streamed down her face. I did not like Mom to be upset. I always wondered why we stayed in those circumstances. My dad could leave out the room and return in a totally different mood.

I heard Dad mention that he had been smoking joints from the time he was a teenager. He grew his own marijuana in our backyard. The weed stunk up our house – drying out bushels hanging upside down in the closet. I barely invited friends over embarrassed of the odor.

Dad worked seasonally at a family business and full-time at the reservation call center. He helped me with my homework daily, and did most of the cooking. Every Saturday, he loved to play jazz on his record player with huge speakers, and he blended up margaritas. I guess the weekend was his time to enjoy himself.

Dad's ex-wife whom he abandoned was upset he got remarried to a younger woman. After he and my mom returned from their honeymoon, she dropped off their teenage son Larry with his belongings. Good gracious, he was a bitter 13-year-old. He would cut the heads of lizards off, and put bleach in my mom's plants to kill them. He would also purposely not flush the toilet after defecating. A few times when Mom went jogging for exercise in the neighborhood, he locked her out and pretended he was asleep when she rang the doorbell.

Larry had a sister named Jill who also came over to stay on the weekends. We tended to battle for Dad's attention.
"Give me some space when Jill comes around," Dad said, attempting to resolve the quarreling.
"Oh, okay," I said, slowly in despair.
"Since you live with me, give us our time alone during her visits," Dad said.
"Yes," I said, nodding as I went to my room and lay across my bed.

As a child, that created a major emotional wound of rejection. I never told my mom what he said. Dad had a deep, intimidating, baritone voice that would scare you speechless. Eventually, he began to take us on separate outings. His ex-wife did not allow me to come to Jill's birthday parties either. As I got older, I occasionally wondered how life would have been growing up if my biological father was alive.

One summer afternoon, we all went skinny dipping at the home of Jack's mother – mom, dad, my step-siblings, his mom that we called Grammy and me. Grammy had a breast removed while battling cancer. As a kid, it creeped me out looking at her jelly breast implant on her dresser. Grammy was sarcastically stern, sort of snobbish, and treated my mother and me like outsiders. She was a conservative lesbian activist. For years, her younger girlfriend lived with her and the local newspaper wrote an article about her entitled, "Little Old Gay Lady."

As a child, I was annoyed when she would walk up behind me forcefully pulling back my shoulders. She made me stand erect against the wall with my chin up, rehearsing walking in a straight line for my posture. I had a minor case of scoliosis, which caused my spine to slightly curve. I always wanted to say, 'Maybe, my posture was never going to be perfect; you mean lady.'

Gradually, my childhood became a living nightmare. Some nights, I woke up during the wee hours crying and complaining that something was sticking me. By the time my parents came upstairs, they did not notice anything. It appeared as if I was whining without a cause. My other stepbrother Greg visited only during the summer breaks and once he was grown up, he revealed that Larry was putting thumbtacks in my bed.

My morbid teenage step-brother Larry began taking his frustrations out on me sexually when I was six years old. I used to sleep with the nightlight on afraid of the dark. I remember seeing his shadow as he tiptoed into my bed slipping off my panties. Once he climaxed ejaculating on my stomach, he would smear it off with a pale yellow towel with swirls on it. I just laid there with a blank stare. I grew to like the sensation but by the same token, I felt confused, violated, and helpless. I had been robbed of my innocence realizing it altered my personality. As a result, I lived in shame as a child. Larry acted as if he was just a pesky big brother in front of my parents. He pretended to be play wrestling with me by twisting my arm toward my back.
"What is your name?" he asked.
"Nobody," I was forced to say.
"What do you do?" he would ask next.
"Nothing," I was obligated to respond, (to get him to stop).
He intimidated me through fear not to disclose the sexual abuse. In addition, it planted a negative seed mentally and was a word curse spoken against me.

Looking back now, I think my dad Jack had PTSD (post-traumatic stress disorder) after fighting in the Vietnam war. When he got upset he would display fits of anger, tear the house up, and chase my mom out into the yard screaming like a maniac. He broke dishes, which caused me to be nervous around this ticking time bomb. I was terrified that if I told about the sexual abuse, I would be in trouble or a ballistic tantrum would occur. Dad slept with a switchblade on the windowsill; I always feared one day he would cut my mom into pieces. I was tormented during my childhood keeping everything bottled up inside.

As a little girl, I recall an incident when there was discharge in my underwear. My mom always did a good job of warning me not to let anyone touch what she referred to as my 'kitty kat.' When she asked me if anyone had touched me, I replied no. I was terrified as she drilled me relentlessly. I lied, claiming I had hit my vagina on the middle bar of my bike. My mom wanted to be certain so she took me to the doctor. I was nervous on my way to the exam. I was praying inwardly that nothing would be discovered. The doctor said my hymen was not broken. It was probably for the best, otherwise, I believe my mom may have committed a crime that would have landed her in prison.

The Lord Stepped In

My mother's life took a turn for the better spiritually. In any case, I never got a lot of spankings, but I noticed a drastic change in her actions. She stopped drinking alcohol, dancing around the house, and using profanities. Mom had obeyed the two scriptures: John 3:5, and Acts 2:38. From that night forward she was a changed woman.

"Let your light shine before others, that they may see your good deeds and glorify your Father in heaven." Matthew 5:16 (KJV)

It was difficult to leave our Baptist roots and embrace holiness as a lifestyle. We were active at our previous church. My mom sang in the choir, and I was involved with the children's ministry. The pastor used to mock people who spoke in tongues. Mom was never striving for spiritual excellence at that church, she was just a 'Sunday Christian.'

We left our old church in adherence to the leading of the Holy Spirit, and moved to The Apostolic-Pentecostal church where she had gotten saved. We became permanent members there. I made friends in my Sunday school class and adapted quickly to our new-found faith. I really liked the Sunday school teacher who had a gift teaching biblical stories so we could understand. I still remember the first scripture verse I memorized that she taught to us as a song: *"Be ye kind one to another, tenderhearted forgiving one another even as God for Christ's sake has forgiven you."* Ephesians 4:32 (KJV)

Within a few months of attending the Pentecostal church, I wanted to be baptized. I understood clearly that baptism was a symbol of the death, burial, and resurrection of Jesus Christ. I was immersed in water in the name of JESUS. Miraculously, after that water baptism in Jesus' name, I was never sexually abused again. A covenant was made over my life. I even suppressed those memories convincing myself I was untampered. I wanted to erase it from my mind and never talk about that shameful subject.

For 8 months, I prayed on my knees after every service seeking to be filled with the Holy Spirit. Finally, I received the promised gift. Speaking in tongues was the most awesome experience. I could communicate with God in a language that I did not learn. My new birth experience was now complete like on the day of Pentecost in Acts 2:4 and 2:38. That was a joyous afternoon for me, it was my assurance of going to heaven. I no longer felt left out in my circle of peers.

In Matthew 18:3 (NLT) Jesus said, "*I tell you the truth, unless you turn from your sins and become like little children, you will never get into the Kingdom of Heaven.*

"Is your daughter's last name Collins?" a member at our church asked.
"Yes," my mom said.
"In a dream, I saw your daughter's first and last name written in the twelve foundations with the apostles," she said.
"Wow! How awesome the Lord revealed her full name to you," Mom said.

Before that dream, she assumed that my mom and I had the same last name, Rivers. Her dream confirmed I was special to the Lord. I always knew there was an assignment to be fulfilled in my life. At a young age, I always dreamed spiritual things. I questioned things out of curiosity and was an analytical child.

My mother always had me with her and her holy-roller friends. I honestly loved going to church. I would call for a ride if Mom decided to stay home from night service with Dad. Coincidentally, a few people lived in Pasadena who were members of the church in Inglewood, Ca. I listened attentively to the sermons and had a Godly fear of displeasing the Lord. I had boyfriends growing up, but I was not fast. If I believed something was not of God, then I knew it was not for me.

I was converted at a young age and became extremely zealous. Inspired, I often talked to my classmates about Jesus. One of my good friends was a Jehovah's Witness. We rode the same school bus together and debated religion. One afternoon, I asked her if we could pray when we exited the bus at our stop. She agreed. I laid the palm of my hand on her forehead saying, "Jesus reveal yourself to her." I was so excited to share this with my mom when she got home from work.

I had friends up and down my block whom I played with, but we went to different schools. My dad used my babysitter's address to get me into Linda Vista Elementary, which was a great school right above the Rose Bowl. From kindergarten through fifth grade, I attended that school. For the most part, going to school there was peaceful except for two crazy incidents that happened in the third and fifth grades. In third grade, an obese girl tried bullying me for weeks. I got fed up and punched her in the eye as she sat at her desk. I was suspended, but she never troubled me again. When I returned to school her black eye still had not healed completely.

In the fifth grade, my teacher flipped her lid on me. She had a stress attack resulting in anger. I cannot possibly imagine what could have upset her so much. She walked over to my desk, took my brand-new Trapper-Keeper folder, slammed it to the floor, and stomped on it repeatedly. My mom visited the school to confront her. The teacher pitifully admitted that she had a terrible day and just exploded.

Troubled Waters

My parents' marital issues continued. Dad was disappointed with mom's lifestyle changes. He wanted the wild, partying woman he ran off with to return. He was no longer happy living with a mild tempered, sanctified, and sober woman. In this case, opposites did not attract. He told my mom she left one day and came back a total stranger.

My dad could be so verbally abusive that he may as well have hit my mom. One time, he stayed out past midnight, and I slept in the bed with my mom. I woke up when I heard him come in and played asleep. He took his shoes off. "Where you been?" Mom asked.

"I been getting booty splattered in my face at the strip club," Dad said, boldly.

I was smart enough to know that his response was inappropriate.

One afternoon while I was at school, a lady desperately banged on our door. My mom answered and encountered a half-naked woman bleeding; whose lips were cut like scissors to paper, her fingers hammered flat, and severe bruising all over her body. Our eighty-year-old neighbor, Mr. Thompson had her held hostage for nearly a week punishing her for smoking up all his crack. Mom allowed her to come in and call 911 for help.

Shortly after that incident, my parents separated. My mom and I went to live with my Grandma Lera who had relocated to Atlanta. We were there for my birthday and had to hide my cake in the trunk. My uncles were strung out on crack, so even my cake was at stake. Grandma Lera was raising a cousin because my auntie had been on crack for years. I was barely ten years old so I easily adjusted. I made friends at grandma's church with the pastor's two daughters who were in my age range. All in all, being away from my dad's unpredictable behavior was a relief.

That short-lived excursion only lasted a few months in Atlanta. The court summoned my mother back to California as a witness to the woman's hostage assault. Unfortunately, my new surroundings were being uprooted to return to my dad. Nothing changed with his conduct; as a matter of fact, it appeared to be worse. His sporadic outbursts of anger resembled a person possessed with demons making his face distorted. He displayed very petty behaviors by hiding the car keys to make us late for church, and chaining the front door when we came home. To wake me up for school he would flick on my bedroom light screaming, "Revelry, revelry, all hands up." My dad would also pour a cup of cold water on me in the shower. He kept me in a nervous frenzy.

Holiday gatherings were a combination of Grammy and her girlfriend, Greg and his boyfriend, and Aunt Sammy and her girlfriend. Homosexuality seemed to certainly be generational in my dad Jack's bloodline. My dad's ex-wife would occasionally attend holiday dinners hosted at Grammy's house. This was an odd setting to encounter as a kid. It was awkward having to deal with all the tension. Nobody knew how to act with my mom and dad's ex-wife both there. My mom's side of the family attended the events, which did help to maintain a balance by adding a humorous atmosphere. My uncles were big jokers and animated storytellers.

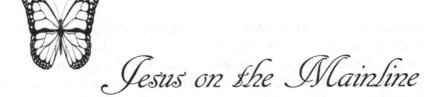

Jesus on the Mainline

We took several kids in our neighborhood to church. I loved sharing the gospel of Jesus, and used to brag to kids how they could talk in a heavenly language. My step-sister Jill got baptized in the name of Jesus and spoke in tongues. Her mom was mad because she did not give her consent.

Shortly after that, the church required parental permission for underage youth that wanted to get baptized. Many young people got saved in our city. We constantly transported car loads of kids and adults to church. Even my Aunt Lynette had to assist us and drive some folks in her car. There were instances they had to make two trips to drop one group off and go back to Pasadena. It was a forty-five-minute commute to gather more people. We were eager to win souls for the kingdom. At that time, the church was near the Forum where the Lakers played.

My pastor's wife, whom they referred to as 'The First Lady' had adopted me in a mentoring program called, 'Little Sisters.' During the summer, I stayed at my pastor's house to attend Vacation Bible School at the church. We were taught the Bible the first week, and the second week we went on field trips. The first lady bought me clothes and invested a lot of her time in me. For our banquets, she dolled me up in beautiful gowns. I spent holidays with them and their three daughters. My pastor's house was an enjoyable outlet away from home. My pastor was always studying the word of God in his home office. He was like a Holy Ghost astronaut, he kept his mind in heavenly places. He lived a lifestyle of 'Holiness.'

Unmercifully Beaten

The City of Pasadena, California funded a new Boys and Girls Club built from the ground up. It was a state of the art facility with a gymnasium, Olympic size swimming pool, kitchen with a dining area, arcade, movie room, arts & crafts, pool tables, foosball, and ping-pong tables. I could not wait for the grand opening in the spring. Finally, the time came and I went to the club during the summer vacation that year. One afternoon, I was sitting on the bench in line waiting to play pool. I was supposed to be the next player in line when a girl walked up and challenged me.

"I got next!" she said, firmly.

"I am next to play!" I said, boldly.

"No, you ain't! I saved my spot and went to the arcade. I'm definitely next," she demanded.

"That's not true, I sat here watching three games. It's my turn! You were nowhere around!" I argued.

"I don't know what you're talking about. My pool game is next," she said, angrily.

"No, you're not. I am!" I said.

I was fed up with her persistence and forcefully pushed her. She flew back 5 feet and then charged at me like a bull. That girl beat me and stomped me unconscious. I was bleeding profusely from my mouth and nose. Finally, I was rescued by the staff and taken into the back office for assistance. My parents were notified and asked to pick me up; I certainly could not walk home like that. I was devastated having suffered such injuries from a childhood fight. Eventually, I found out she was a 14-year-old in foster care. She happened to be short for her age, stocky, had a chipped front tooth, and uncombed hair. She probably took every bit of abandonment that she felt out on my face.

My dad's boxing lessons did not work for me. He used to make me punch the palm of his hands as a target. He showed me pressure points to push, one was in between the thumb and index finger and the other between the neck and the shoulders. Nevertheless, the military training he passed down to me was no use during this brutal attack.

Both of my eyes were black, my entire face was bruised, and my lip was swollen for weeks. I felt ugly like a monster. That incident gave me a phobia of fighting. In my mind, I never wanted to be beaten like that again. I felt awful as if I had been in a car accident. My dad was so attentive to my injuries as he iced my face every few hours. The swelling eventually left, but the bruising was still there. My mom had to put foundation make-up on me so I could go to school, but that only hid my outer scars. I could find nothing to take away the mental and emotional wounds. The angry teenager did a number on me and my self-esteem plummeted even further. At eleven years old, I felt like a defenseless nerd.

Teen Things
& Drama Scenes

My hormones were out of whack before my 13th birthday and I was agitated. One afternoon, I got so upset with my cousin Calvin that I almost strangled him to death. All I remember is sitting on top of him in our front yard choking him. My mom and Aunt Lynette looked out the window and had to dash outside to pull me off him. A week later, my menstrual period started while at school. I was not surprised because my mom had spoken to me over the past two years about how the body changes during puberty. I went home to tell my mom that 'it' was here.

As I turned thirteen, the Lord gave me a clear revelation of His calling on my life. I always wondered why God would not allow me to fit in. I had genuine passion for church and the activities surrounding it. I kept good grades simply because I was naturally smart, and I did not want to be on punishment. I wrote term papers revolving around religion. My English teacher marked up the paper with a red ink pen and called my mom asking why I did not choose other subjects.

I had a Caucasian teacher named Mr. Donnelley. He tried to be more like a friend to students in this predominantly African-American middle school. He would buy underprivileged kids tennis shoes and students looked up to him like a hero for his actions. One day, he hypnotized a few students as if he was some magician. Most of my classmates were amused by others barking and displaying abnormal behavior under hypnosis. I thought it was improper. The same week, Mr. Donnelley decided to show a movie with soft porn by Monte Python. I told my mom about the hypnosis and the nasty film, so she rented the movie over the weekend. Appalled by what she saw, she notified the principal first thing on Monday morning.

Mr. Donnelly was fired because he was not supposed to hypnotize students or show R-rated movies. It was later discovered he was a pedophile. He had a history of molesting children at previous campuses in other states. The kids he financially supported became upset with me. I was bullied and chased home from school. My schoolmates were so bold, they threw rocks at my house. My dad was going to fight them, but of course they ran away when he went outside. In the last semester of eighth grade, having to switch schools was a major inconvenience. My previous school was directly across the street from my home, and now I had to be driven to a neighboring city. I graduated from middle school with strangers.

As a teenager, we used to get dropped off in groups down to a huge block party. Pasadena was the home of the New Year's Day Rose Parade. I looked forward to a festive night on the town. On New Year's Eve, people camped out partying in the streets all night. They sprayed silly string, danced, and celebrated. All glory to God I was not kidnapped in that large crowd without my parents. It was freezing around 4 AM in the morning, and I called home for a ride.

My first year of high school was awkward. I felt like an alien because everyone was so advanced. I was used to church friends with good values and morals. Suddenly, I was exposed to a fashion show with wild teenagers. I only cared about how I looked going to church. I had no sense of fashion as a tomboy. I wore business skirt suits with a low heel on Sundays. Otherwise, I did not know what was in style. My biological father was very conservative, so I was not much of a risk taker with fashion.

I had one close friend from middle school named Shelley who lived in walking distance. My dad would pick her up every morning and drop us off to high school. We tried out for the basketball team and made it through the physical conditioning training referred to as 'hell week.' Shelley was a very talented athlete. She played point guard on the varsity team with junior and senior players and was the team captain. I was placed on the junior varsity team starting as small forward. Shelley was light skinned, with sandy brown hair, and very physically developed. I suspected that the basketball coach had a crush on her.

After basketball practice, I was calling for a ride home on the pay phone outside of the girl's locker room. I saw a girl from afar taking off her sandals and handing them to a friend. She ran uphill toward the locker room. I turned my back to finish talking. 'Wham!' she hit me without notice. I dropped the phone and my first instinct was to run, so I sprinted down the pathway to the office.

My childhood phobia from being beaten unconscious was back. I was scared to even attempt to defend myself. I wanted to prevent those types of injuries from occurring again. Later, I discovered that she attacked me because she was jealous over a boy she liked who was interested in me. Truth is we were not even dating, he was a typical player who made advances to all the girls. I think his intention was to see if he could have sex with me. After that incident, I never entertained his conversations.

In the tenth grade, I started to have a desire to fit in with the crowd and struggled with the call of God on my life. Deep within, I knew I would never be the cool kid per se', because I had a goofy sense of humor. I was not having sex, smoking marijuana, or attending weekend parties like my classmates. People knew something was different about me, and they teased me by calling me 'church girl.'

In my chemistry class, we were doing an experiment. Like a dummy, I set a paper skeleton on fire that was attached to the bulletin board in the back of the class. I was unaware we could have blown up with the chemicals in the classroom. Someone told on me. I was at risk of being expelled from the school district. I was so afraid of the consequences that I told my first big lie, and stuck to it as the truth. My step-grandpa intervened in the situation. I was able to stay at my high school without any repercussions.

Culture Shock

During the second semester of tenth grade, my parents had divorced. My mom had always worked in Los Angeles doing hair, so she decided we would move closer to her job and our church. She was skeptical of taking me to the inner city, but I wanted to live with her. We relocated to a nice community for upper middle-class black people. After service, we saw a member from our church at the store. Her name was Lona and she invited us over for dinner. From that day forward, she was like an aunt to me. She became 'family' in every aspect.

We had also moved near our pastor's house. This was very convenient for me since I already spent a lot of time over there. I was an assistant to the first lady, which is referred to as an 'armor bearer' in the church arena. I was the only woman on the security team. We waited outside in the parking lot for the pastor and the first lady to arrive. The men would gather his belongings, and I would take her coat, hat box or other items out of the car. Once she was ready to make her grand entrance into the sanctuary, I escorted her to the row that the pastor's family occupied. I also accompanied her to church conventions.

Unfortunately, I ended up walking in a spirit of pride, allowing the first family's loftiness to rub off on me. As a teen, I overheard things that I should not have. I was advised by the first lady not to disclose what transpired in their home. I never even told my mom their business or private matters about other members at the church. I was brainwashed into thinking that my loyalty remained with them. When their daughters reached adulthood they had cars, jobs, and got married. I was a bridesmaid in all their royal weddings.

The flip side of this move to Los Angeles was that the school in this area's district was rowdy. Inglewood High School was a culture shock. It was just like the movie, *Lean on Me*. I began to skip school because the environment was hectic and I stuck out like a sore thumb. A fight broke out every other day mostly between Black and Hispanic gangs.

A shopping plaza was across the street with a burger stand and several people would go there during lunch. I noticed students would ditch school and play video games over there. I made friends with the cashier and started cutting class visiting him. Occasionally, his brother would pass through to order food. One day Lorenzo, the cashier's brother, invited me to ride with him to run some errands. After that, we hit it off like buddies. He picked me up in the mornings from the burger stand to ride around all day.

The day that my Aunt Lynette went into labor, Mom came to pick me up from school. Sure enough, I was not there. The administrative office told her I had not attended classes in over sixty days. The school was so unorganized they never called home to notify my mom. I was busted, and I had some explaining to do now, but I kept it real.

"I dread going to school, Mom. It's nothing like Pasadena. This chaotic school has me afraid to go to class," I said, desperately.

"I did not know it was that bad. You should have said something right away. Well, I am going to take you out of that school," she said.

Surprisingly, I was not required to repeat the tenth grade. However, when I returned, they arrested me. My mom was lost for words seeing me put into the back of a police van. I was responsible for reporting daily to the continuation school in the rear of the campus bungalows. It was worse than the actual campus; it was for pregnant teens, truancies, and those who fought.

Luckily, I was taken out of the wild high school that I ditched half the semester. My mom enrolled me in a diverse school with beautiful surroundings in Culver City. After one semester in eleventh grade, I talked my mom into transferring me to another high school. My friend Mike from church attended Westchester High School and his mom volunteered to give me a ride.

My high school track record was so inconsistent, it's a miracle I received a diploma. Mike and I had a crush on each other, but it was gone in a heartbeat. He began dating another girl who used to visit our Sunday night church services. I was hurt that he did not want to date me after admitting that he liked me. I told him off for misleading me, and we stopped speaking after that argument. A while later, Mike messed around with a childhood friend at my church who was effeminate since we were kids.

I was the typical book worm focused on my education, but I despised school. It was tough waking up on Mondays after being at church sometimes until midnight. All I was looking forward to was graduating from high school. I regretted jumping the gun and switching schools because I was stuck at Westchester High School. It was predominately Black with kids from well off backgrounds focused on fashion. Once again, I did not fit into this environment.

After my first season, I decided not to play on the basketball team. To my surprise, there were lesbian team members who I caught kissing in the locker room. Basketball is an aggressive sport that causes young ladies to have a manly disposition. The sport mentally influences you to be tough so that you will be ambitious to win. Squatting down in a defensive stance, boxing out for rebounds, and guarding your opponent was like being an ape on the court. There is no way to be dainty or act feminine playing such a viciously competitive sport. Many enter into homosexuality by playing because the devil uses women's basketball as an entry for gender identity battles.

Church Hurt

One year, I shared a room with a camp counselor at the youth retreat. After one of the panel discussions, I was praying on my knees in our hotel room. The young lady came in and jumped into the shower with her boyfriend. They never noticed me kneeling next to the bed because they went directly into the bathroom. I quietly hid under the bed in shock. I really looked up to her like a mentor. That was a little disheartening to discover that she was putting up a facade at the church. Months earlier, the pastor had spent a portion of the bible study dispelling a rumor that she was pregnant. I assumed that the rumor was a slanderous attack, but now I was seeing things in a different light firsthand. I had witnessed so much in the church. I was beginning to wonder if the people were worshiping God or the leader.

My church was affiliated with a large Pentecostal organization. There used to be an annual summer convention for young people. It was held in Palm Springs, Ca. where the desert temperature stayed in the 100's. We spent most of our time swimming. This was the first year that I went without my mom.

The kids of some of the other pastors' stole a golf cart, went joyriding around the resort, and wrecked it as the security chased them. Somehow, we managed to buy wine at the store, I poured mine into a soda can. I rode with my friend Kathy who had just gotten her car in twelfth grade. The organization was not allowed to return after that year. Our pastor canceled the upcoming events for our youth department, and rebuked us over the pulpit before he preached.

I loved the church more than anything. I had become attached to the First Lady, and the physical church building in the aspect of it being a social club. I had a reverence for God, but my spiritual relationship was not solid. I was looking for the validation of man instead. I helped at weddings, set up for game night, and assisted in the kitchen. I had no idea what was going on in the world outside of the church walls.

I maintained a 3.8 GPA all throughout high school. I had high expectations of being an evangelist working in the vineyard for the Lord. My pastor sponsored me to attend an adult accredited Bible College. I was the youngest student to enroll while still in high school. There was no doubt I wanted to be in full-time ministry. My youth leader asked me to speak at the Christmas dinner for the young people. I admired a world renowned, prolific speaker named Dr. Iona Locke. She visited Los Angeles frequently, and we took a beautiful photo together at a convention. My desire was to have a ministry as impactful as hers when I grew up.

Three of my childhood friends from church were inseparable like the three musketeers. Angie, Lynn, and Kathy were always cool with me; we just did not hang out often. I pretty much interacted with my peers during our youth activities. Kathy was the one in the group I had more of a connection with. I was mature for my age, but not fast. My mom was a cosmetologist, so she kept my hair done and my first lady even gave me a few of her Chanel designer handbags. In high school, I was mistaken for a college student because of my demeanor and style of dress.

For some time, Angie had been vaguely hinting that she had a crush on a married minister who was twenty-six. I thought it was silly of her, but I just brushed it off and gave it little thought. One evening, I drove my mother's car to take my final exams for Bible College, I stopped by the church afterward. I was sixteen at the time and had my driver's license. This night, Kathy, Angie, and I were in the fellowship hall talking.

"I have a secret to tell y'all. You cannot tell anyone," Angie said.

"Well, spit it out. Angie, what is it?" Kathy asked.

"Yeah, I am curious," I said, at the edge of my seat.

I had no clue what she was going to say.

"I am the babysitter for Minister Berry and Trisha because she works nights. Minister Berry and I have been having sex. I am in love with him," Angie said, naively.

"What! Oh my gosh! Girl that is crazy. You are going to get in trouble with God. He is married sis. He is not going to leave his wife. This should never have gone so far," I said, perturbed.

"Angie, I knew you liked him, but I never imagined all of this. I think you should stop going over there," Kathy said, concerned.

"You guys don't understand. We love each other. I should be his wife. I am going to keep our relationship a secret. Minister Berry is my boo. Besides, he knew I liked him, and he married her anyway," Angie said, blushing.

"This sounds like a bad idea. You are going to get your feelings hurt," I said, with certainty.

"Well, we will see. Everything is wonderful," Angie said, in denial.

We wrapped up the conversation and went to sit inside the sanctuary to hear the choir rehearse. Twenty minutes later, Minister Berry yanked the door open, standing in the doorway frowning, and beckoning our attention. His hands were on his waist, his shoulders were squared, his legs spread apart, and the jacket was swept to the back like a superhero's cape. We gathered in the first lady's office. I still was not sure why we had been summoned until Minister Berry spoke.

"What is being said?" he asked, in an intimidating manner.

Present in the office was: his pregnant wife, the first lady, Kathy, Angie, and me. Just as quickly as Angie confessed to us someone overheard it. There was a room connected to the fellowship hall, so I believe an eavesdropper had been sitting back there during Angie's confession. I walked out storming across the front of the church during choir rehearsal. To avoid a scandal behind my pastor's back, I went and tapped on his door.

"Come in," he yelled.

"Praise the Lord, Pastor. There is some confusion going on that you should be aware of. It's a meeting being conducted without you. This is a serious matter," I said, upset.

Pastor called on the intercom to his wife's office.

"Hey, bring this meeting to my office," he said, sternly hanging up the phone as five adults and three minors gathered in his office.

"Somebody heard you guys talking. What is going on?" Trisha asked, angrily.

"Yes, what kind of lies are circulating?" Minister Berry asked, firmly.

Angie looked flabbergasted. My heart raced as there was a pause of silence.

"What do you mean?" Kathy asked, timidly.

"Who said Minister Berry is messing with Angie?" the first lady probed.

Our pastor stared from behind his desk with his glasses at the end of his nose, and looking over his lens. His head was bowed and his mouth opened – puzzled.

"I do not know," Angie answered, emphatically.

She was fourteen and had just expressed she was in love with Minister Berry. I know she had not planned to reveal her secret. Her body language was saying, 'Whatever!' It was as if she was on the witness stand.

The first lady was trying to over talk everyone and downplayed the story.

"I think this is a false accusation all blown out of proportion," she said, since Minister Berry was like a son to her and our pastor.

"I believe this story," I insisted, becoming frustrated and wanting the truth to come out.

"No! No! No! This is hearsay," the first lady said, in defense.

"Let her finish talking," Pastor said, abruptly rebuking his wife.

The first lady looked embarrassed and rolled her eyes at me. I was defending my friend since I was two years older than her.

"I don't think this should be overlooked," I continued.

I thought Angie would ultimately expose Minister Berry since he supposedly had committed statutory rape.

"Is it true?" Pastor asked Angie directly.

The room was filled with tension. Minister Berry looked at her with a pleading expression. She was paralyzed with fear and in distress, she took a moment to respond.

All eyes were on Angie as she shook her head, "No."

"Drop it and do not discuss it again, do not tell your parents either," Pastor said, fuming with anger.

I felt the situation was not handled properly. A pastor's obligation is to shepherd the flock. He should have covered us better. Discernment is a gift that comes through the empowerment of the Holy Ghost. I believe he dismissed the matter for the sake of the church's reputation. Sometimes good pastors make bad decisions.

My mom was worried all evening wondering why I had not returned in her car. She called the church, but no one answered the phone. Cell phones were not common at that time. I had a pager device. Finally arriving home, I was a nervous wreck.

"Where have you been?" my mom asked.

I could not gather my thoughts right away.

"I was at the church, something happened. I want to shower and put on my pajamas," I said.

I was very upset and needed to calm my nerves, praying under my breath to relay this story to Mom. Once I disclosed this information my mom was lost for words. Due to the mental anguish of her recent divorce she was under duress. When I told her that the pastor said not to tell our parents, she never addressed the issue. Our pastor tended to blast people from the pulpit and breach confidentiality laws, so my mom was reluctant to say anything. I was on the blacklist now. When I arrived at church I no longer had my position as the first lady's armor bearer (security).

"We will get her belongings today," the head of security said.

"Oh okay," I replied.

I went to sit on the second row reserved for the first family. When the first lady marched out of her office, I felt her negative vibes. Nevertheless, after church I greeted her.

"Pastor said you cannot sit on this row anymore because you fell asleep while he was preaching. You need to sit further back now," she said.

Her disposition was offensive as she slung her hair with her nose in the air.

Ironically, later that same day, I ran into the pastor in the lobby.

"What's wrong? You look discouraged," he said.

"The first lady said I cannot sit on the row anymore because you said I fell asleep," I lamented.

"Huh, umm, let me talk to her. Don't you worry about that. Cheer up. Get you some joy daughter," he said.

His expression revealed he was bewildered.

I had witnessed the backlash toward other parishioners, but I never imagined my turn was coming. "The first family" acted like the mafia in church. If you upset them, your name was on the hit list. The word would spread, and others would ostracize you too. I went to church the following Sunday. The first lady's cousin was the usher who stood at the back door.

"The floor is full," he said, as he blocked the entrance.

"Oh," I said.

My mom always sat on the front row working with the baptismal ministry. We had no choice but to sit on the balcony after the usher claimed the seats were all full. It felt strange because we had never sat up there; it was designated for people with children. It so happened that my mom ran into the first lady in the restroom during service. They stood side by side at the sinks to wash their hands. My mom greeted her, but the first lady did not reply. She flipped her hair and exited.

Every New Year's Eve, the church had communion and foot washing service. Everyone came out to that service desiring to renew their commitment. My mom worked late that evening to finish her clients so we arrived at church a tad bit tardy. Again, the church was packed. My mom did not think the first lady was still upset, so she suggested I sit on the family row as usual. As I was ushered to the second row, the first lady looked up at me, dramatically waved her index finger gesturing 'no' and turned her head. The row had plenty of empty seats.

Embarrassed, I went to sit in the balcony. I was appalled that she could treat a teenager with such animosity, holding a grudge against me. She had groomed me from childhood, sponsored my prom with a beautiful silk Swarovski crystal dress, and assigned my date. My childhood bond with her appeared to be breaking, and our relationship was taking a turn for the worse.

I was excited about my high school graduation. Since I started kindergarten at four years old, I was about to graduate at seventeen. I asked the first lady if she would be in attendance. She told me to set aside five tickets for her family. I assumed that meant she was accepting me back into the circle. Some of my own family members were counted out trying to accommodate the first lady. A day before the ceremony, she canceled.

"My daughter said it would be unfair to support you and not attend all the other church members' graduations," the first lady said.

I could not understand how that mattered all of a sudden. The 'first family' always had their favorites, being a respecter of persons. I was crushed with disappointment. My relationship with God as a young person was not stable enough to endure the emotional abuse. These kinds of traumatic events are referred to as a "church hurt." It had become one thing after the other; I was fed up with the church. Once I lost the first lady's affirmation it destabilized me.

High School Prom and Graduation

Plot of the Enemy

My mom could no longer afford our $1,200 house rent. Thankfully, the salon owner where she worked rented us a two-bedroom house he owned. God gave my mom favor. There was no security deposit was required. He just wanted the place occupied. We lived rent free for three months and only paid $650 monthly thereafter. We moved across town to the Miracle Mile area near the skating rink called "World on Wheels." This area was crazy, off Pico Blvd and Redondo Avenue. A gang rivalry was prevalent during that time. All we saw was yellow tape surrounding homicide scenes. The only convenience was that my mom worked five blocks from our house.

I had no intention of returning to my church, and tried to masquerade the inner hurt that I felt. I did not want to think about the rejection that I was suffering from. Somehow, I began calling this party line for entertainment in search of new friends. I planned to do a little networking with the world. You could go through about twenty rooms to chat with people. They did not have trending social media platforms then. I met this dude named Slow Poke who was flirting with me and I thought he sounded cool. In my state of boredom, I agreed to meet him in person. I drove over to his house like an idiot to meet a stranger. For all I knew, he could have been a serial killer. I got to Slow Poke's door and it was wide open.

"Hello, hello," I said.

"Come on in," someone replied, echoing from the back.

Directly in my eye's view of this studio apartment was a guy laying across a bed asleep. He was handsome, light brown complexion, with a curly top tapered haircut, and medium build. I assumed he was my date. I figured, maybe he dozed off because I took a while. Initially, I was so excited thinking the party line had a good catch for me. After I entered the small home, the young man sat up, and had breasts. I was shocked, not sure if this was a prank.

The plot thickened when I was approached by the real guy walking out of the bathroom looking horrific. He had two ponytails, a sunk in face, with bad acne cratered skin, long dirty nails, and two rows of cluttered teeth. I was so outdone trying to keep a normal expression on my face. I should have run out the door.

The Devil was about to change my entire life starting today.

I thought to myself, 'What in the world is going on up in here?' The one I found to be attractive was a lesbian woman. The person I came to meet resembled Rocky Dennis in the old movie called "Mask." Obviously, this was not a love connection so I made up an excuse why we could not go on this date. I claimed to be stopping by to meet briefly. We just had some small talk. In the urban LGBT community, the tomboy lesbian is referred to as a **"stud."** Her name was Tandy, and she was friendly. We hit it off socially, and she invited me to a club the following week.

"I swear, it's jumpin' and celebrities are there weekly," she said, with enthusiasm.

"Wow, are you serious?" I asked, with childlike excitement.

"Yeah, it's the most popular club on Tuesday nights," she said, convincingly.

"I definitely want to see what the hype is about," I responded eagerly.

She made this club in Hollywood sound like I did not want to miss it.

Every day thereafter, I began to hang out at this run-down studio apartment. The stud Tandy was dating Slow Poke's sister, and it was actually her place. She was not there my first time over, but I met her the next day. The girlfriend Brianna was a stripper who worked a lot while Tandy smoked marijuana, drank alcohol, and played dominoes all day.

I left home with my backpack pretending I was going to secular college every day. Instead, I drove my mom's car over to this new hangout anticipating this club. I started drinking alcohol, puffing a little marijuana, and playing dominoes too. I was eager to see some celebrities and determined to make it to this nightclub. Many days, my mom worked at least ten hours. I would fail to pick her up sometimes causing her to have to walk home.

Tuesday had come around quicker than I thought. I was making my debut to this lesbian club called Peanuts in Hollywood, Ca. I got picked up early in the day by Tandy's friend. We were meeting up for a cocktail party. I began to smoke a lot of marijuana to calm my nervous jitters. I drank some cheap liquor called MD 20/20 guzzling down a 24-oz. bottle.

I had never been drunk before. The intoxication took me by storm, and I became nauseous and dizzy. I walked toward the front of the building and leaned over the balcony vomiting straight liquor. That was a clear indication I needed to go home, but the devil was on an assignment. Everyone insisted that I would be fine.

"Throwing up is the remedy to a speedy recovery," Tandy said.

"Ugh, I feel out of it," I managed to say faintly.

With their assistance, I got to the car still discombobulated. We were piling up in a soapbox compact Nissan Sentra. In total, six of us were in the car; two in the front, three seated in the back, and I was laid across their laps as the extra passenger. I was feeling sleepy and desired to get dropped off.

"You are going to be fine. You need fresh air so we will keep these windows down en route," Tandy said.

Twenty minutes commuting to Hollywood, I was cold and desperate to get out of this cramped car.

On arrival at Peanuts, which was located at 7969 Santa Monica Blvd, I felt slightly sobered up. I was ready to explore the new scenery. It was a long line as we crossed the street. Tandy knew the promoter, so we went to the front opposite side of the line's velvet rope for VIP entry. I was underage so by entering with them, I bypassed being carded. The only men permitted entry into Peanuts were celebrities who were required to wear suits. I was impressed by Tandy's clout. I decided that night that I would be hanging with her more often.

As we entered, I felt like, 'Wow, I'm seventeen and at a real nightclub.' It was awfully dark in there only the disco lights were spinning around. I heard the roaring crowd of people cheering for the stripper sliding down the pole. The first eye-catching scenery I noticed shuffling through a crowd of onlookers was the spotlight on the VIP booths. I recognized several celebrities sitting up on the back of the booths with bottles of liquor on the tables. A lot of thriving women in the industry were present too. I was like a kid in a candy store gazing around. The place seemed so cool to me with all this excitement. My adrenaline was pumping and the fascination of my surroundings was alluring.

I met men and women who were nice to me. Somebody bought me a drink at the bar. A few people wrote their numbers on napkins passing them to me. One girl I met randomly struck up a conversation.
"Hello, my name is Amanda. Do you party here often?" she asked.
"Nope, it's my first time here."

As a conclusion, we exchanged numbers. My friends and I had separated. Once the strip show was finished, I located them on the dance floor. We jumped up on the stage. Out of nowhere two girls sandwiched me and started to grind on me. I was the new face in the place so they were coming out of the woodwork. Suddenly, some other studs (tomboy lesbians) started throwing up gang signs. My friend Tandy was tall and hefty like a man. I guess she did not like that the other studs invaded our space. She punched one of them and the other passengers who rode with us jumped into the fight. My first night out a big brawl broke out. It was chaos, I got out of the way paranoid someone might blind side me.

Turned Out

I called Amanda a few days later to see how she was doing. We talked a while sharing a little bit about ourselves. About twenty minutes into the conversation she asked, "So are you gay?"

I paused, gave it some thought.

"Not really. I was invited to the club, but I've had no previous encounters with women."

"Me and some home girls were trying to meet celebrity men. I have not slept with a woman either, but I was attracted to you when we met," Amanda said.

I was speechless, but I played it cool.

"Oh, it sounds like we have something in common," I laughed, nervously. I did not want to make anything seem awkward.

"Let's hang out sometimes. Are you willing to visit Bakersfield?" she asked.

"Sure, why not? I have not been there before. I don't have my own car so when are you coming to Los Angeles again?" I said.

"My roommate wants to pick her nephew up in LA this weekend, so does that fit into your schedule?" she asked.

"Sure, I will see you then," I said. We hung up, and I wondered what I would say to my mom about my weekend getaway.

Amanda and her friend drove to the city to pick me up. I spent the weekend at the campus apartment they shared. I had no idea what our friendship would produce but I was open minded. She barbecued and made some mixed alcoholic beverages in the blender. We listened to some music and eventually her roommate went to sleep. I took a shower and Amanda got in afterward as I was putting on my pajamas. I wondered what the sleeping arrangements would be, but figured she would let me know.

Amanda came out of the shower in a towel and dived across her bed. She said, "Let's cuddle." I was nervous; however, the liquor gave me a sense of courage. I felt a sensual comfort as we embraced each other. I used my imagination to figure out the rest as to what lesbians do. We turned each other out. Engaging in lesbian sex for the first time was a huge experience that both of us explored, and we were no experts.

Amanda was girlie and I had a tomboy streak from my athletic upbringing. The two weeks of hanging around Tandy, I knew I wanted to be the man in the relationship. The weekend was interesting as we felt like our lesbian virginities were taken. We went to the mall and had frozen yogurt. The next night, we drank again and were intimate.

"Tandy, I am gay now," I said, grinning on the phone.
Tandy laughed and asked, "Hey, did you like it?"
"I did, but I need some pointers from you later," I said.
I did not want to go into details on the phone. I would wait until I got back to Los Angeles to continue talking to Tandy.

Homosexuality is unnatural lust, but the eroticism and emotions can be misinterpreted as normal.

When I returned home, my mom still thought I was leaving in her car to college every day. I continued hanging out with Tandy and another stud named Devin. They knew each other from high school. Slow Poke was like a friend now. Surprisingly, he had a girlfriend all along. Daily, Amanda and I talked and she really wanted us to be a couple. I was okay with the idea, but I was clueless as to what I was signing up for being curious. I reckoned it would not be smothering because she lived two hours away. Here I was, after my first gay rendezvous, in a relationship with a female.

Tandy was too big for me to fit her clothes, so Devin let me borrow a shirt to wear to Peanuts. I was hooked on that club – it was calling my name again. The rapper Jay Z wrote about Peanuts in his song called, "Give It to

Me." The lyrics said, "Same song I'm back been around the world romancing girls that dance with girls from club Cheetah to club Amnesia to *PEANUTS IN LA* bubblin in Dublin's." This spot was so notorious it made headlines in a song. It became a thirst trap for me.

Amanda was a college student so she periodically came to Peanuts. That gave me the opportunity to meet other ladies. I was learning the ropes awfully quick. Tandy and Devin had a lot of low budget girls they conversed with. I wasn't fond of their referrals playing matchmaker. I think Tandy only lived with her girl because she was using her for financial gain. We had plenty of time to run the streets because her girlfriend Brianna was always gone shaking that money maker. Brianna was the first person I witnessed sniff lines of cocaine. I thought she was wild, but that was her prerogative.

I think Amanda and I had only lasted two months, it phased out quick. I wanted to mingle with all the women who came weekly to Peanuts. The next one I met came with benefits. She started braiding my hair in corn rows. She had a job and bought me men's clothes. I thought I was big pimpin' now. I was developing my image. My mom was baffled as to why I stayed gone so much. Every chance Mom got, she dabbed blessed oil on me praying.

I started introducing myself to girls as Jamil since Tandy and Devin were using alias names that were unisex. Moment by moment, I was being seduced into this lifestyle. I no longer was concerned about anything pertaining to religion. A few people tried to contact me from my church, but it was too late. I already decided I wanted a taste of the world. I thought it was nice of those who made the effort. Some of them called on the phone, and others even stopped by my house. Particularly, neither the 'pastor nor his wife' ever reached out to me. That was like pouring acid on an open wound.

Minister Berry's wife, Trisha, found a love letter from Angie in his suit jacket months later. It no longer mattered to me if the truth had come out because I was sucked into the "gay scene." Sadly, a crime was not reported.

Minister Berry is the only one who apologized to Mom later about that situation causing me to backslide.

My behavior and appearance were becoming progressively worse. I was learning masculine behavior and met more gay people as the days went by. All the studs I started hanging around connected me to other circles of lesbians who were **fems** (a term for feminine lesbians). I was becoming well-known in the gay circuit. For the first time, Devin and Tandy came by my house to pick me up. I let them meet my mom introducing them as my male friends. They passed for guys easily, so she did not suspect anything otherwise. My mom expressed a major concern because I never had friends outside of the church. Clearly, their rough appearance was not a crowd I would have associated with prior to my church hurt.

My mom was very disturbed at this point by my bizarre change of appearance. I took all my church clothes, smashed them into the corner of one side of the closet, and covered them with a sheet to make room for my new wardrobe. I gathered all my church literature, Bible college textbooks, and anything associated with God to place them in shopping bags.

"Mom, I don't need these anymore," I said, nonchalantly.

She looked stunned as she took a deep breath.

"What do you mean?" she asked.

"I gotta go my ride is coming," I said.

It was not up for further discussion, and I put up a wall. My life turned into one big party overnight.

2 Pac Took My Girl

Devin and I began to establish a friendship hanging out alone. We were single, and Tandy had to tend to her relationship sometimes. We went over to a young lady's house named Keisha. We smoked marijuana and had a few drinks. I thought Keisha was a nice person. I was introduced to another club called the "Catch One." Since I was underage she offered me an I.D. to get in. We exchanged phone numbers and planned to go that Saturday together. Coincidentally, it was two miles from my house straight up Pico Blvd. It was the only black gay club around. I had never heard of it before until then.

When Saturday got here I decided to jump on the bus early, which was a straight shot to Keisha's house. She planned for a friend to pick us up. I was really fascinated by this huge club. It was spacious and had an adult entertainment strip show. I could not believe there were so many gay people that existed in Los Angeles. My horizons were swiftly broadening. I met a stripper named Velvet who slid me her phone number. I was excited, only eighteen, but feeling grown meeting an older woman.

The club left a striking first impression on me and sure enough, I got tipsy that Saturday night. It was too late to get the bus back home so I spent the night at Keisha's apartment. We were both so intoxicated and horny, we had a sexual encounter. I was young and silly, I burst into laughter on top of her. She was around twenty-four years old and did not see the humor in anything. Keisha's fictitious porn dialogue rattled me into silliness. There was no sexual chemistry between us, so I never went that route again. She remained a friend from then on and became like a big sister.

I thought I was a trophy piece, but, I was just fresh meat. I got turned out for real with that stripper. We went to the novelty shop to buy a strap-on, which is a plastic penis and harness to hold it in place. Velvet was an advanced sex partner who showed me all the tricks of the trade. She was my first 'soul tie.' I asked her to be my girlfriend, and she consented. I dropped her off to work and picked her up a couple of nights a week from the strip club dancing for men.

2 Pac, the notorious rapper came to Peanuts one night. As the security escorted him in, I was in the walkway that he had to pass through to get to VIP. I had become a fan of his music as I pursued my rebellious lifestyle. My girlfriend Velvet and her other stripper homegirl Chocolate were gold diggers and preyed on men with money. They maneuvered their way later into VIP to seduce 2 Pac and his producer. At the end of the night, they accepted the offer to leave the club with them. Velvet pulled me to the side in front of the club.

"Babe, we are going with them. I will call you tomorrow," Velvet said, effortlessly.

"Oh, okay," I said, with a blank expression.

"Let me introduce you to him."

"Alright, cool."

"Pac, this is my girlfriend."

"What's up? Good to meet you," 2 Pac said, with a grin.

"You too man," I said.

"Alright ladies, let's go," 2 Pac said.

The valet pulled up in a luxury car as I watched her get in. I hung my head in shame as she pulled off. I was honored to meet him, but he was dashing off with my lady. I quickly became aware that the lesbian scene was all about a good time and opportunity. Peanuts was known for celebrities coming to meet freaky women. Shortly after that incident, Velvet and I broke up. I faced the reality that she was a cheap thrill. She was not the kind of woman who could be in a monogamous relationship. I was naive, caught up in the heat of passion, and tender-hearted. My experiences began to shape my perspective.

$\mathcal{F}ive$ $\mathcal{E}leven$

I met my first gay male friend at the Catch One nightclub. His name was Ramone, and he was friendly at the bar. He spoke a language of his own.

"Hey girl, what's the tea? What you givin' tonight?"

"What's up?" I replied.

I was not quite sure what that meant. (Later I discovered it meant what are you up to).

"Who you here with honey?" Ramone asked, in a cool manner.

"My friend Keisha and I came together, but who knows where she wandered off to?" I said.

We got our drinks from the bar and walked around the club. From that day, we grew to be good friends.

The following week after I met Ramone, he invited me to hang out at his best friend's apartment. His best friend was a transsexual who looked exactly like a woman. I had never seen anything like that before. If he did not tell me, I would have been fooled. Her name was Savoya. She was light skinned with a beautiful face and feminine curvy figure. Savoya had a roommate named Coco, who was in the beginning stages of transitioning. I knew at first sight Coco was not a real woman. Coco was extremely tall, brown skinned, had a blonde bob cut, and no breast implants at that time. They both did hair as a profession at home.

Their apartment was always filled with customers and friends. Everyone piled up on their sectional couch smoking marijuana and cracking jokes. A variety of gay people ranging from gay boys, tranny's (the short term for transsexuals), studs, and fems would be there. We all made harmless fun of each other, which was called "reading." Gay men had their own ways of communicating called "the gay lingo."

I got along well with one tomboy named Chili that was not gay then, but eventually crossed over. She was a mixture of Black and Hispanic. From the day we met, she became a loyal friend. I seemed to fit right in with this crowd because I was funny and loved to laugh. I really enjoyed how carefree they were with no stipulations as to how one should behave. They called the apartment hangout "Five-Eleven," which was the address of this downtown residence by Alvarado Park.

We started going to the Catch One during the week just for drinks and shows where drag queens lip synced. I had started drinking daily. I spent nights out at their apartment, and bought enough clothes to last just to avoid going home. The gays were like a family circle of acceptance. I dropped out of secular college in pursuit of my new identity and the lifestyle I chose. Anything different seems to be exciting, so I got caught up in the moment. I was young, energetic, and without experience looking to be adventurous. Women paid to take me out on dates. They bought me cologne and clothes so my wardrobe was expanding rapidly.

First Gay Pride

I remember my first Gay Pride weekend at Zuma Beach in Malibu, Ca, 4th of July weekend. My friend Q, a college student on a basketball scholarship invited me. I met her while dating Velvet, and Q was dating another stripper. We did not hang out often due to her schedule, but we had our memorable times. That day, we wore some Nike swim trunks, with the shirts to match, surf shoes, and hit the beach. We had long silky flat-ironed hair (called a wrap).

Lots of gays who were in their late twenties and early thirties were there. As new faces, we got lots of attention, but the other studs did not receive us well because we were a threat. We had careless attitudes, trying to get all the phone numbers that we could. Thousands of people were at the beach. Many had tents on the sand, vendors were selling food, and some were sunbathing. It was a huge stage was set up with a DJ blasting music. A body contest for men and women was held and there was a booty shaking dance-off with prizes awarded to the after party.

We went to the after party that night held at a hotel ballroom, but we had to linger in the lobby because we were not old enough to enter. So many people were hanging out, and we blended right in. This was such a huge event that out-of-towners flew in to attend. People invited us to their rooms to have drinks and smoke marijuana. We had a full night of adventure with strangers. Shortly after Q returned to college in Georgia, she was murdered by her girlfriend's ex-boyfriend. I was devastated losing my friend. That was the first gay person's funeral I had attended, and it would not be the last.

The Glory Departed

A few months later, right before my 18th birthday in November, I was visiting "Five-Eleven." A gay barber named Joey, lived on the floor beneath Coco and Savoya. All the gay boys got haircuts from him that Tuesday. Everyone was getting ready to go to a bar in Inglewood, called the Caper Room. I was admiring their fresh cuts.

"I want my hair like Todd's when I decide to cut it off," I said.

"Do it now," Coco advised.

"I am afraid of my mom's response to this drastic measure," I said.

Before I could ponder on it too long Coco was pressuring me.

"Jamil, come sit in my chair I got you."

"I don't know about this Coco. I had better wait," I said.

"Don't put off tomorrow what you can do today. You are grown. Your mom will get over the shock either now or later," she said.

Coco took the clippers with a guard on it and mowed my hair off.

A Bible verse says, *"Isn't long hair a woman's pride and joy? For it has been given to her as a covering"* (1 Corinthians 11:15 NLT).

My glory departed as my full head of hair was now on the ground. She handed me some money.

"Go downstairs and let Joey fade it up and line it professionally," she said.

Joey had great talent. He gave me a bald fade and texturized the top to make it curl up. I was a satisfied customer. It was official like the referee with a whistle. I looked like a totally different person. I had become transgender overnight, which is defined as someone whose gender differs from the one they were given when they were born.

"Satan desires to sift you as wheat" Luke 22:31 (KJV)

I was going in the opposite direction of God's standards wanting to appease my lustful desires. I looked like one of the fellas literally passing for a young teenage boy. I was tall, slim, and barely had any breasts. My underdeveloped body was always an insecurity. My logic was it's no sense in having a ponytail with men's clothes on. I leaped into the deep head first, bypassing any shallow water. That is to say– I wasted no time. It was like a 'coming out' party all over again.

The bar we went to that night had all gay men who mistook me for a boy. They inquired about me. Many of them were highly disappointed when they discovered I was not a man. I seemed to be the highlight of the night. Most studs and gay dudes' personalities usually clashed. The gay men acted like females, and the studs impersonated men. It seemed to be a conflict of interest. I just liked to have fun, treated everyone with respect, and I expected the same.

The next day, I went home while I knew my Mom was at work, apprehensive to face her with my hair cut off. Coco offered to let me stay with them for a while, so I gathered about two weeks of clothes. After a few days, I called my dad to ask if I could move back to Pasadena.

"Hello, Dad, I want to move up there. I am gay now and my hair is cut completely off. Mom is not aware, and I am not trying to deal with her right now," I said.

"Pasadena is always home baby. You are welcome here, but your mom is going to be worried about you disappearing on her," Dad said.

"Thanks, Dad. Yes, I know my mom is going to take this hard, but I will call her soon," I said.

Dad was accustomed to homosexuality since his mother, sister, and son lived alternative lifestyles. He raised me since I was four months old. I loved him. He is the only father I know, especially after the loss of my biological father Skip as a child. I knew I could go back to Pasadena and be welcomed with open arms.

I appreciated the offer from Coco to stay there. Nonetheless, I did not want to wear out my welcome. She took me home again, this time to get all my clothes. I moved out to my dad's house while my mom was at work. He was in that huge house alone. May as well be where I could have my own room, opposed to staying on a friend's couch.

I planned on being wild since my Dad drank, and smoked marijuana throughout my childhood. I should have known my Mom was not going to allow my great escape to last. She came the next day to see why I left without telling her anything. When she arrived, I was upstairs.

"Honey, you might want to sit down," my dad said.

"Why would I need to sit down? She needs to come from up there," my mom said, demanding.

I overheard them and strolled down those stairs making my grand entrance with an attitude. A spirit had overtaken me for real. I had a new walk, look, and mannerism. The big, baggy, hip-hop look was in style then, and I wore a sports bra to flatten my chest. I was no longer intimidated by what I thought Mom would say.

"WHAT!?" she screamed, buckling over and grabbing her chest.

I thought she was going into cardiac arrest. It reminded me of the TV show when Fred Sanford would grab his heart yelling, 'This is the big one!' My attitude was, get used to it this is me! My mom was paralyzed with shock.

"You don't look like yourself. Where is my daughter?" she asked, in disbelief. "You need to come home," she pleaded.

"Nah, Mom this is what I'm doing right now. See this is my new look," I said.

She hid her face in the palm of her hands. I went back up the stairs continuing to get dressed. Eventually, after my dad consoled her, she left.

My best friend from middle school, Shelley, moved in with my Dad. Her mother had moved to Ohio. Somehow, she flew back with her newborn baby. The father of her son lived in Pasadena, but they never reconciled. A stripper ended up turning out Shelley. She began to wear men's clothes and chopped her hair off too. You could tell she was a woman because of the way her body was shaped, and she was wearing oversize hoop earrings with lipstick.

A few weeks after staying with us, Shelley lied on me and told my Dad I tried to have some men rape her. I did not know why she would conjure up such a crazy story out of the blue. My Dad seemed to believe her. He scolded me over those false accusations. I was outdone by their nonsense. I knew I had made the wrong choice by moving back to Pasadena.

I was disgusted with the living arrangements with Shelley's whining baby. I was gone as much as I could, busing it back to Coco's house. One night, while I was gone, Shelley got drunk, fought with somebody in the apartments down the street, and a car ran her over. She survived with a broken femur bone and several scrapes. My Mom and I went to the hospital to pray for her. Alcohol was reeking out of her pores. Her speech was slurred and the pain medication also had her out of it. I could not stand to see a long-term friend injured.

I had no idea that Shelley was an alcoholic. For the two years that I had moved to Los Angeles when my parents divorced, we did not stay in touch. Shelley would become belligerent when drinking. Her actions caused me to steer clear of her even in the same residence.

After receiving an income tax check, Shelley bought a car. Tandy and Devin came to Pasadena with some females to hang out a couple of times. Shelley became my ride to the club. Riding with someone who was drinking and driving was not the brightest idea. Her car was a long, old, raggedy, yellow 1970 Cadillac Fleetwood. It was too big for her to handle. She would swerve all over the road.

One night, Shelley had an emotional meltdown that scared us to death. She began to talk about her unproductive life, her stripper girlfriend who was avoiding her, and the responsibility of motherhood. Tandy, Devin, and I

58

tried to convince her to pull over and let one of us drive while she vented. She refused. She became psychotic – slamming on the brakes. Then she pulled out a pocket knife and cut her arm. We were spooked. Blood was dripping onto her clothes as she ranted and drove recklessly. She stopped at a red light, and we all bolted out of the vehicle on foot toward Tandy's house. Shelley tried to run me over. Her car ended up crashing into the porch steps of a neighbor's home.

The Lord truly had angels watching over me.

Shortly after, Tandy, Devin and I parted ways because Tandy's girlfriend had a crush on me. Her girl was just desperate to try a new partner since Tandy was her first female. I did not want to be in any drama, so I stopped going around them. Tandy was a husky stud, and I did not want her pouncing on me behind her lover. I subtracted myself from the equation.

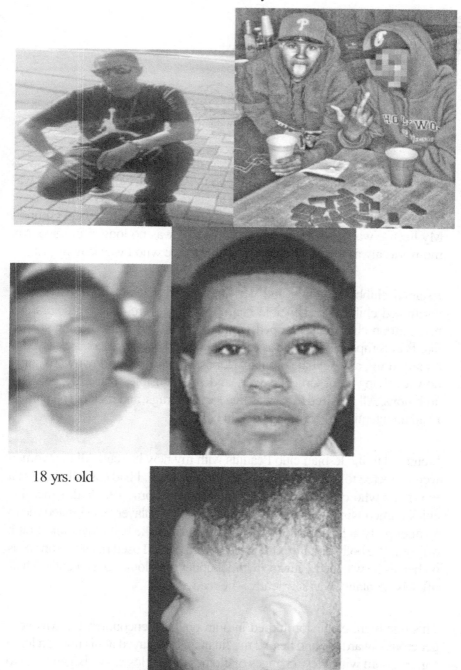

18 yrs. old

On the Battlefield

After feeling endangered around Shelley, the inner city of Los Angeles was calling my name. Nothing was going on in Pasadena. Not having a car was a challenge and it seemed impossible to get rides. Eventually, I did go back to live with my mom. I began meeting people from all types of backgrounds. My license was suspended, but getting a ride was no longer an issue. My mom was always looking out the window to see who I was leaving with.

I started clubbing nightly and was introduced to ecstasy pills. The pills resembled children's chewable vitamins. They were different colors and had cartoon characters stamped on them. Then they started being shaped like Bart Simpson's head, four leaf clovers, and transformers. Ecstasy was a party drug, and sexual stimulant. I was officially on a downward spiral now evolving into someone wild and irresponsible. I had no goals or ambitions. All I desired to do was live for sex, drugs, and rock n' roll parties. I had no intention of enrolling back in college.

I returned to the lesbian club Peanuts with my new haircut. All the women were attracted to me like a fresh face all over again. I had casually known a few folks who complimented me on how handsome I looked. I met this chick named Nina who was with a famous NBA player. She invited me to an after party at his mansion. The professional basketball player and I hit it off well. We both took turns having sex with Nina. I used my strap-on penis on her, as he watched. I always wore it under my clothes once I cut my hair off. My mentality was stay ready – be ready.

This one-night excursion turned into an ongoing encounter. He was very generous toward me and helped me financially. I stayed at his house a lot in a guest room with a few changes of clothes in the closet. We began to go to Peanuts together recruiting other women to have orgies. A lot of the strippers indulged in cocaine, so I began to sniff it also. Eventually, I could buy a substantial amount of cocaine to become a dealer. I was climbing the ladder of popularity. I was hanging with a well-known player on the Los Angeles Lakers team, and I had the drugs.

My parents reconciled and got remarried on New Year's Eve in 1996 because my Dad got saved. I did not think that was a good idea. My mom had just buried her brother, and I had shaved my hair making my homosexual declaration. I think as she was grieving and vulnerable she made the decision hastily. She was also listening to other people say it was God's will. Dad moved in with us, and now they were double-teaming me. They made me re-enroll in college, set a curfew, and tried to stop me from getting high. I was not easily persuaded to conform to their rules. I did not make curfew and came in when I well pleased.

Santa Monica Blvd. in Hollywood, Ca. was the stroll where transsexual prostitutes made their coins. *"Coins"* is the gay lingo word for money. Anywhere between La Brea to Western Avenue was the strip they walked to solicit dates. The donut shop on the corner of Santa Monica and Highland was open 24 hours. My tranny (transsexual) play sister named London started having me look out for the police while she worked. I liked the idea of being out all night on the block.

Once I saw how things went out there, I decided to get on the bandwagon. That corner had at least a hundred people in the parking lot, where there was also a novelty shop. Many people turned tricks or did drug transactions inside the sex shop. I broadened my drug distribution business to accommodate all the addicts. I had crack cocaine, crystal meth, ecstasy pills, powder cocaine, and marijuana. So many other gay people migrated up there because of their families kicking them out behind their lifestyle. I was hanging out up there voluntarily, refusing to comply with my house rules.

There was never a dull moment up there all night. Celebrities would pick up transsexuals, which began to shed light on the *"down low"* brothers; a term for undercover homosexuals. Also, a lot of the transsexuals had boyfriends who were so-called straight dudes. That is called *"trade"* – an urban, gay lingo term for a dude who is possibly in gangs, or married to a woman, but he does not go to gay clubs or associate with gay people per se'.

I rented cheap motel rooms a few miles from Hollywood in Silver Lake. I slept, changed clothes, and packaged my narcotics. I had grown accustomed to sniffing cocaine not realizing I had a habit. To maintain some type of high, I started taking the remainder of the crack shavings and lacing my marijuana with it. That was the worse decision I could have made because the high was so unbalanced. It had me in a sketchy frame of mind where I was irately aggressive. Marijuana makes you relaxed and crack keeps you awake. That combination is referred to as a *"primo."* Smoking 'primos' reminded me of how people described nodding off on heroin.

Sometimes, I would blackout on the bus going to my parents' house. One night, the bus driver woke me up tapping me saying, "Last stop, you gotta get off." I was way in Malibu, Ca. – at the end of the line. Initially, I was only supposed to go five stops, but I blacked out. I was stuck at the bus stop in front of a well-known restaurant named Gladstone's. I stretched out on that bench, went to sleep with two cell phones on my hip, jewelry, money, and drugs on me. Nobody but Jesus looked after me on that busy street called Pacific Coast Highway. True enough, it was far from the ghetto, but deranged people are everywhere.

I woke up in the afternoon with the radiant sunlight in my face, discombobulated and trying to figure out why I was there and how. I was surprised my yellow special edition Nextel phone and other belongings were untouched. I crossed the street to travel in the opposite direction toward home feeling grateful, but rested. The streets were taking a toll on me staying up for days.

My parents attempted to lock me in the house to clean up my act. I was there probably for two days. I finally disclosed what I had held in for a lifetime buried in the back of my mind. I broke down in tears trying to get my words out.

"Larry was having sex with me as a child," I said, trembling.

"Oh no. I used to dream of a shadow in your bedroom doorway. I felt in my gut something was wrong, but you never told me," Mom said, tearing up. My dad Jack sat there listening.

"Well, it happened. I cannot hold this anymore. Let me out of this room. I need some air!"

Now that it was all out in the open, I felt a sense of relief and crawled up in their bed to go to sleep. It was not handled correctly. My dad called all his family. They denied that could have ever occurred. My step-aunt even confronted me on the phone one day when I answered. My dad wanted me to sit down and discuss it with my step-brother Larry, but I was not comfortable seeing him. My other step-brother Greg did not doubt it, neither did my step-cousin Carl that I was raised with.

"If you do not want to have a family meeting about this, then I do not want to hear anything else about it," Dad said.

I cussed out my dad. Finally, I stood up for myself for the first time. That was the most ridiculously hurtful remark. After I mustered up the courage to tell a childhood horror story, he had the nerve to tell me that. Nothing was ever resolved, but I was free in the sense of not keeping a dirty, little secret.

I ran from my confession feeling awkwardly shameful in the same house with my dad. I began to wander to friends' houses in search of solace. Sometimes, my mom would come up on Santa Monica Blvd on her way home from church. She begged me to come home. She could not understand why I would be on the street with homeless people. After a while, Mom began to walk the streets passing out church tracts.

It was like a posse up there that would look out for one another while hustling. I got addicted to fast money that I was not working hard for. After a while, nobody wanted powder cocaine, so I dropped that product for the time being. I slacked up on going to the club Peanuts. This new environment was entertainment and cash in one setting. I discovered a new club called the Arena on Santa Monica Blvd within a block from the donut shop.

I began walking up on Hollywood Boulevard and Sunset Strip selling crack and meth. Several tourists and addicts were in Hollywood. The street value in the ghetto for a ten-dollar rock was sold easily for twenty dollars in Hollywood. I was making a nice amount getting double the money for my products. I tucked my money under the sole of my tennis shoes or Timberland boots. The Mexican gangs ran things up there in Hollywood, Ca., called 18th Street and White Fence. If they caught you on the side streets you would be in trouble. They jumped out of vans robbing people and beating them up. Also, if you wanted to avoid any trouble, you had to voluntarily pay taxes to a dude they called, "The Lieutenant."

I spent the daytime hours in the dining area of Carl's Jr. on the corner of Sunset and Highland. Today, that location is a Chick-Fil-A franchise. The dining area was indoors, but it was separated from the counter with the cashier. I sold crack all day out of that fast food restaurant with no hassle. I ordered a meal and sat waiting until sundown to begin my foot patrol.

I remember my first time seeing the Lieutenant. I was standing with some other dealers in front of McDonald's on Hollywood Blvd and Highland next to the Wax Museum. All you heard were people whistling down the block screaming, "The Lieutenant is coming!" I was aware of the rules not to be caught on the side streets, but I had never seen him. My buddy who called himself "No Name" said, "Let's go inside." People literally began to disperse at the alert of the Lieutenant's presence. Being nosy, I hesitated. I observed from a distance one Mexican dude surrounded by bodyguards paired in twos at the front, center, and rear of him. I did not budge as he stopped when he got in front of me.

"Are you working?" he asked.

"Nope, I'm hanging out trying to catch some tourist chicks. I'm a lesbian," I said. He looked at me with a smirk.

"You are funny," he said. We shook hands. "Come on, walk with me."

They let me walk beside him in the assembly line as we conversed. The men with him collected fees from those selling drugs. He had a slight limp as if he had been shot in the past. The Lieutenant was around 6 feet tall, had a low haircut, and a huge Roman numeral tattoo on his neck. XVIII was the visible tattoo for his gang Eighteenth Street.

He trusted my vibe so much he took me to his penthouse. We smoked marijuana and I admitted to him that I did slang dope on the 'tranny ho stroll.' He gave me permission to sell drugs in his jurisdiction with no taxes. The gang members did not go on Santa Monica Blvd. imposing on the gay people. They harassed heterosexuals in the areas that were considered their gang territories.

"If anyone gives you trouble, tell them the Lieutenant Rico is your comrade," he said.

"Alright, good lookin' out. Thanks, Lieutenant," I said.

From that day, I had access to Hollywood. The 18th Street gang hated Blacks, but I got a pass.

I was introduced to Downtown L.A. by some other hustlers in Hollywood. When business seemed to slow down, they would hop on the train. We went Downtown to sell our crack. I started going back without them. That was the capital for homeless crackheads, but they were cheap. They would offer you $3 in change if you would accept it. Money did not add up in $20 increments like in Hollywood. The police's presence was much more visible down there also due to the high crime rate.

I started feeling sorry for the homeless people and brought old clothes and jackets to them. I have always been concerned about the well-being of people. One day, a stranger walked up to me.

"What are you doing down here? You're standing out like a sore thumb," he said.

God was speaking through that man. It was dangerous to be down there by myself. Anything could have happened to me. There were tents along the sidewalk and makeshift housing out of cardboard boxes. After that man approached me, my eyes opened. I realized being there was a safety hazard. Downtown L.A. was a short-lived excursion that lasted less than a month.

My Grandma Wyatt was battling cancer. I was going to see her in the last stages of her life. It was sobering to watch her in that state. My mom and a friend that I called Aunt Maggie went to pray for Grandma. At the end of her life, the Lord was so gracious to fill her with the Holy Ghost speaking in tongues. She had been baptized in Jesus name years prior. That was a true 'deathbed confession.' Shortly after, Grandma Wyatt passed.

Rest in Paradise Grandma Wyatt

A Miracle on Meadowbrook

One day, I met two brothers at the liquor store on the corner of my street. They asked me where they could find marijuana. Since I had it for sale they 'lucked up' that day. I lived on Meadowbrook, which was closer to Pico. They were new to California from Maryland, and lived with their mom and other siblings on the opposite end of Venice Blvd. They became customers and smoking buddies when I was in the neighborhood.

Most occasions, I connected with them at their house. Their mom was cool and young acting. They had a married big sister in a wheelchair with a two-year-old baby. After building a rapport with them, they told me their big sister was not born disabled. The mom had referred to a settlement before, but I did not know any details. Later, I was informed that the sister had fallen on a broken step in their apartment building and became paralyzed. Her husband seemed so patient pushing her around the house.

I had been out about three days selling drugs and smoking primos (marijuana laced with crack). I needed a break from Santa Monica Blvd. and got an early bus home. My mom decided to hide my phone so that when I fell asleep nobody would disturb me. I took a warm bath and became extremely emotional in the water. I immersed myself backward underwater and came up speaking in tongues and prophesying.

"The Lord wants to heal the disabled woman," I said, urgently.

My mom busted into the bathroom to see what the commotion was about. I was crying.

"Mom, get my phone we need to call these people; the Lord wants her to be walking for her baby," I said.

My mom was clueless as to who I was talking about. She quickly followed my instructions and we called them up to come over right away.

It was raining on that gloomy day during a storm called El Nino. They agreed to stop by. Within ten minutes, they pulled up at the front of the house. They drove a minivan that had a sliding door on the side. Instead of bringing her out in the rain, we met them by their vehicle. My mom proceeded to give her ministry background.

As my mom stood talking with a small bottle of blessed, holy olive oil, the paralyzed lady's mom said, "I am a backslider. I am Holy Ghost filled, and I know about that anointing oil."

I reached across my mom whom I felt was moving too slow, and laid hands on the young lady.

"In the name of Jesus *Talitha cumi*. Be healed," I said (Mark 5:41 Aramaic interpreted "damsel arise").

Everyone was silent and in disbelief. I moved so boldly with an unction of power that was felt in our presence. Tears swelled up in everyone's eyes. They hugged us.

"Thank you for the prayer. We had better get out of this rain," the mother of the disabled lady said.

Within the hour, they called back to testify and rejoice that she was taking steps in their living room. Wow! Awesome God! I never saw them again, they moved shortly afterward.

My Celebrity Chick

Santa Monica Boulevard had been under heavy surveillance after a few assaults, complaints from business owners, and even solicitors of prostitution being robbed while dating. Too much activity on the 'tranny ho stroll' caused extra patrol cars to circle the blocks and back streets. I got stopped on a bike one night with a mouth full of crack rocks lined between my top lip and gums. I was inwardly scared that I was going to jail. I swallowed some of the crack rocks by accident. Luckily, I had them wrapped in plastic; otherwise, I could have been poisoned. The police officers did not find anything on me. I was released from their harassment mistaken for a boy. They claim their reason for making a U-Turn was because I had no front light at night on the bike.

That close encounter with the law had me paranoid, so I took a break from up there. I decided to stop selling meth and crack because the only customers I had were up in Hollywood. The marijuana and ecstasy pills were still could generate some money from home. I was hooked on the 'primo high' not realizing I was smoking crack myself. I thought it had to be in a glass pipe for me to be considered a smoker. I had become accustomed to this rare taste when I put it in the weed, fascinated as it sizzled. I now wanted to keep that high going – chasing a euphoric numbness.

I asked some young dudes that would beg for change at the gas station where they bought crack from. I even offered to buy them a dime rock for the referral, so they escorted me to the door. They took me around the corner to a spot which was an upstairs apartment. I got my twenty-dollar rock to crush down to roll. I was not going clubbing without my fix. I was on a mission accomplished.

I was so high one night, I sat on the steps of a shopping center stairwell by my parents' house on La Brea and Pico. The two young guys who were homeless began telling me their life stories. One had a mama who was on crack, so he got on it following her footsteps. The other one was raised by his grandmother who died. He said depression and no place to go drove him to drugs as an escape. They were both in their early twenties. I wished I was twenty-one to legally buy alcohol and enter clubs without a fake I.D.

I had smoked my primo, but desired to continue my binge. I had more crack and no weed to roll with it. They offered to share their pipe, so I tried it. The high never kicked in as I kept lighting it, waiting to feel something. They said hit it, hold it in, then blow it out. All I remember is getting frustrated because I did not get high. I am grateful that my addiction did not progress into puffing a crack pipe. That one night could have taken my life into a darker direction than it was already headed in.

"I know the plans I have for you, says the Lord. They are plans for good and not disaster, to give you a future and a hope." Jeremiah 29:11 (NLT)

One night, after being a frequent customer at this new crack spot, I went on my way to get the bus to Hollywood. I always kept a fresh haircut, new clothes, and the latest sneakers that were out. For the first time, the spot was closed and nobody came to the door. Surprisingly, the apartment across the hall had its front door open.

"Hey, what do you need?" I heard a voice yelling through the gate.

"Let me grab a dime," I replied.

When the woman came to the door to make the exchange, she looked me up and down. She could probably tell from my anxious behavior, I was not an undercover cop.

"You too young and fly to be smoking dope, my nigga," she said, concerned.

"Oh, this is for somebody else," I lied.

I walked away feeling ridiculous and realized I was too young to be messing with crack. However, I still got high that night and took the bus to Hollywood. Shortly afterward, I stopped rolling my marijuana sprinkled with crack. I realized how out of character I was behaving with unexplainable blackouts and an invincible attitude.

I always ran with people who were known to be fighters, even in the LGBT community. When it pertained to the street life, I ran with gang members who were dangerous. I never witnessed a murder or committed one. I had respect in the streets contingent upon people knowing the company I kept. Although I lived a life of crime, I attempted to persuade other people to make better decisions with their future. All along, I should have taken my own advice. I enjoyed what I was doing, but did not realize how time would fly by me.

Sometimes, I would sell crack out of London's motel room, (my tranny play-sister) I was hanging with on Santa Monica Blvd. Her boyfriend was from a gang called Compton Piru, and he was my security. Their room was right by my parents' house on La Brea called the 'Relax Inn.' Her car was being repaired, so I was going to drop her off on the ho stroll. An altercation broke out between a crackhead and someone else. The guy started shooting. Immediately, I ran. He stood over the staircase shooting downward. The crackhead was two steps behind me running down the staircase. He was shot. I could have sworn I got hit. I sat in my car patting myself to feel for blood. I stopped going to that death trap.

God had an angel assigned to me that I could not see.

I had not hung with Shelley after she tried to run me over with her car that night. She was living in Los Angeles, and now hooked on the crack pipe. She stayed with her own father who abused crack since we were younger. I assume he got her on it, but her actions had been questionable for quite some time. Strung out, shortly after staying in an area called the 'Jungles,' (where the movie Training Day was filmed) Shelley was murdered. The word on the street was she owed money for drugs. Somebody drop kicked her down a flight of steps, and she broke her neck. I could not believe this happened. Although we grew distant, I was heartbroken the way her life ended prematurely. An old schoolmate on our basketball team got custody of her son in Pasadena. I guess Shelley's mother did not want the responsibility of raising a baby. The Lieutenant, from Hollywood in the 18th Street gang was murdered too.

I met a stud who looked just like a rough dude and was flashy like a rap star. We were at the 'Catch One' night club flirting with two fem girls in the bathroom line.

"Aye what's your name?" she asked.

"Jamil," I said.

"I like your style, let's link up. I don't fool with nobody, so this is a privilege. My name is Rocky," she said.

"Thanks, man," I said.

Rocky got my number and walked out.

The next evening Rocky called and said to be ready in an hour. It was on a Sunday, which was the day that car clubs took their low riders onto Crenshaw Blvd. That was the cruising strip where thousands of people came out to show off. She picked me up in her Buick Grand National with triple gold Dayton rims. All the thugs had those rims on their cars at that time.

Pretty women would pack up in cars to meet men on the strip. We both passed for dudes, so we were about to blend in where we could fit in. Rocky was a Blood from East Side Family Swan. She was on the TV show "Cops" as a gunshot victim. A rival gang member blew her eye out, so she had a glass eye. She wore expensive shades a lot. I knew from the first time we met she was a real gangster. I became worse off than I was once I met Rocky. I wanted to be just like her. She was about 6 years older, so she influenced me a lot.

We were a force to be reckoned with at the club. Most studs had visible breasts and we didn't, so they were jealous because we passed for boys.

Rocky had an older friend who was a stud named Domino, a gang member from Inglewood Family Bloods. She showed me a lot of love and put me on with a bunch of marijuana before (gave me drugs to sale on consignment).

Rocky had another buddy who was taking 'weight' (large quantities of drugs) out of town. She made plenty of money from investing in that operation. My first time going to Las Vegas, Rocky took me for a fight weekend. Las Vegas was so crowded I was amazed. We fooled women and revealed our real gender later. Being gay was not so popular in the late 90's. Straight women tended to cuss you out in public if you approached them.

I did not manage the money well, and we smoked the marijuana up in Las Vegas. I was trying to figure out what I would tell Domino. I thought one of my girlfriends would give me the money, but I ran into her before my chick got a paycheck. Instead of shooting me, she snatched me up in a choke hold.

"Blood, you're like a relative, I don't want to F--- you up. You cannot do bad business. Don't let it happen again. I'm trying to keep money in your pocket just slide me mines," Domino said.

"Alright, my bad – I understand," I said.

I was an irresponsible square peg trying to fit into the circle with no street knowledge. I learned the principles of the thug life, the importance of respect in this drug game, and how to manage responsibly. I was fortunate that Domino did not hurt me. There were no misunderstandings from that day forward.

Rocky took manipulating women to another level. She taught me that pleasing women was just like acting, so keep the frame of mind that I am trying to win a Grammy. That was the best advice she could have given because I no longer got caught up in emotions. I was strictly in it to benefit from these ladies. She showed me how to be like a rude dude and boss women around. Rocky had a pimp mentality that began to influence me to set a $500 quota with women before I slept with them.

"Listen it ain't cool to perform oral sex on women. Real gangsters make hoes get on their knees to give us head. That's how you really turn 'em out," Rocky said.

Rocky was tired of being on the run after avoiding a court sentencing seven years prior. She decided to face her fate to clean her criminal slate. They only sentenced her to three years because she had not been in any trouble. I hated to see my friend who was like a big brother to me leave. I remained a loyal friend by writing her updates on the happenings in the streets. I was representing the gang neighborhood wearing red all the time. I thought I was a tough guy running with all these notorious thugs.

I hung out a lot at the barber shop on Pico, a block away from my mom's house. I had a barber with the nickname 'No Limit Les' from New Orleans. I was like one of the fellas. It was an illegal operation because nobody was licensed, but they were skilled. The decor was a hip-hop shop with graffiti art on the walls and stickers on the floor. They gambled all day rolling dice on the back patio. When it closed, we drank and smoked marijuana all night.

The liquor store was next door at the corner of my street. They liked joking all the time. They gave everyone a nickname, that's how I got my name, which stuck with me for the rest of my reign. They said I looked like the rapper Nas. Since he had a clothing line out called Willie Esco, they named me Esko. I spelled it with a 'K' since my crew was Bloods and I avoided using the 'C' like Crips. The barber shop dudes were not in gangs, they just liked to smoke marijuana and cut hair for a living.

I had a gay friend named Trey that I started going over to his house to play video games. I was eighteen, and he was twenty-five with his own apartment. I was only smoking marijuana without anything laced in it. I was no longer in Hollywood all hours of the night. After a while of being around him, a chemistry began to grow between us. I was attracted to the feminine qualities that he had. He was initially going to allow me to penetrate him with my strap-on penis. He complained that it was too big, so he did not allow me to fulfill my fantasy.

One night at the gay club, while sitting down he sat in my lap and kissed me. I went home with him and experienced my first sexual encounter with a man aside from being violated during childhood. It was a little uncomfortable in the beginning, but I never imagined that intercourse with the opposite sex could be enjoyable. He had never been with a female either. He could not look down below my waist because he had to visualize me as a male. We were both nervous as he concentrated on my face to keep an erection.

My Mom and I were always close, so I told her about Trey. The part that I left out was that he was gay. She thought I was going to be straight now. All that experience did was cause me to be adventurous. Trey ended up being a player who put up a good front in the beginning. He became jealous and threatened a girl I was dating. I thought since we were both gay, it would be no issue. Then he became physically abusive. Domestic violence is used to gain power and control over another person.

Low self-esteem will cause you to settle for what you know in your heart is unacceptable. Being controlled by emotions is a form of witchcraft.

I ended up busting this other stud leaving Trey's apartment. I was coming from a job at a temporary agency. I recognized this stud from the club because she was dating a tranny (transsexual) at the time. I figured that after his first heterosexual encounter with me that Trey was making his rounds now. I was outdone by him and took the opportunity to cut ties after I caught him with the other stud. That was a short-lived, overbearing relationship.

Perversion makes people freaks and opens doors to other things once you cross into the abyss. Most women who alter their appearance into a masculine presentation; are damaged from childhood sexual abuse, so they don't feel attractive, and suffer from rejection. God placed it in a woman to desire a man. I had so many void areas in my life that I was in search of love and attention in emotionally unstable environments.

I saw the tranny named Delight, who was dating the stud I caught leaving Trey's house, alone at the club. I told her what transpired, and she told me that she found Trey's phone number in her girlfriend's pocket weeks ago. She was not surprised because she mentioned her stud girlfriend was also sleeping with a male neighbor in their apartment building. We decided to exchange numbers to compare notes.

I discovered that my experiment with a man was not rare. Regardless of how lesbians may portray themselves, some of them do sleep with men. Several have given birth to children as evidence. They conceal their heterosexual encounters because sleeping with the opposite sex is considered a violation of the gay lifestyle. How twisted is that to be ridiculed for what is the natural order of God. The world's perception of things can be warped. If everyone was gay none of us would have been born.

After having sex with Trey, some lesbians tried to tarnish my reputation. I viewed those who were gossiping as judgmental. In my human nature, I was practicing my free will. Boundaries cannot be created when the acts are all against holiness. There are no rules when you are committing sin.

For man did not come from woman, but woman from man; neither was man created for woman, but woman for man (1 Corinthians 11:8-9 NIV).

Delight broke up with her stud girlfriend and moved out because of infidelity. Her new residence was in Watts, Ca., around the corner from the Nickerson Gardens projects. Delight was thick, very ghetto, and she fought a lot. We became close after several months hanging out smoking marijuana.

Delight rode with me to pick up a half pound of marijuana one night. By this time, I was selling it solely for myself with no responsibility to split the revenue. I had just moved into my own apartment in Leimert. I exited the 110 Freeway coming down Vernon Avenue westbound toward Crenshaw. As soon as I got to 8th Avenue, we were pulled over. I moved quickly, stuffed the marijuana down my pants, and prayed the officer would not smell it. I was hoping that the butts in the ashtray would be mistaken for the odor. The officer walked up with his flashlight.

"License and registration sir," he said.

"Officer, I'm a female. Please allow me to get my wallet from my back pocket, and the paperwork out of the glove box," I said, politely in a ladylike tone.

I always changed my voice when encountering law enforcement. Soon as I handed it to him, another squad car pulled up beside him. My heart dropped again. I just knew they were going to follow usual protocol by calling a female officer to search me.

"We got a stabbing. Let's go!" the other officer yelled, with urgency.

"Have a safe night," he said. He handed back my documents.

I was relieved from thinking I was literally going to jail. If I had been asked to step out of the car, I'm sure that huge bulk would have been obvious. Thank you, Lord Jesus is all I could say.

A few months later, I was dropping Delight off at home in a gang neighborhood called 'B-Bop Watts.' My back window got shot out soon as I pulled in front of her house. I think the guys across the street, three houses over, had been watching me for a while. I was coming over there wearing red all the time, from my hat to my shoe laces. That neighborhood's gang color was blue for Crips.

The bullet was lodged into the door panel two inches from Delight's head. I believe it must have been a double barrel gauge shotgun because the hole was the size of a nickel. That shook me up, and I stayed out of that area for a while. By the time I resurfaced, I was always in rental cars. I was getting an accelerated course on the streets. I had not been gay for long, and things were happening rapidly.

I met a young lady who was an actress co-starring in a popular sitcom. The club Catch One was the lesbian hot spot on Saturday nights, called "Puss N' Boots." This young lady had her friend approach me.

"Excuse me, are you here with somebody?" she asked.

"What do you mean?" I asked.

I was cocky with a smart mouth. She was not my type. If she was the one trying to get acquainted, I was going to decline the offer. Women can be so cunning, they waited until my friend Keisha went to the bathroom to approach me.

"Well, my friend is wondering if that's your girlfriend?" she asked.

"No, she is my sister," I said.

"Can I introduce you to my friend?"

"Sure, it's cool."

Keisha walked back up and I debriefed her before they came over.

"You know who that is right?" Keisha asked.

"Nope, who is it? She looks like a regular person to me." I said, laughing.

"Fool, that's the girl on this television show," Keisha said.

"Oh, for real? Well, I had better jump on that sis. Here they come – shhh," I said.

She was introduced to me as Courtney. We exchanged phone numbers. I called her the following day. She had a great personality. Ultimately, I turned her out. She told her parents I was a boy. We were both eighteen in the club with fake I.D. We started spending the weekends in North Hollywood at my friend Ramone's house. I used to go on the set for the filming of the show. The star of the show would flirt with me because she and Courtney were rivals.

Courtney did not know how to drive. My license got suspended, so her friend would drop us off to the valley for our weekend rendezvous. We both started talking "the lingo" like two flaming gay men from being around Ramone. This girl had to be getting a nice salary on a highly rated television show, but her parents controlled all her finances. She was only given $100 every weekend. Her parents wanted to make sure she did not get carried away splurging. My whole intention of gold digging was thwarted.

Her personality grew on me and the publicity of dating her boosted my image. She woke up drinking cheap alcohol for breakfast. The kind of generic liquor that did not have a name it just said, "Distilled Gin" in a plastic bottle. She would get drunk and want to have sex all day. We never went anywhere outside of the gay club. Her career could not be jeopardized by her parents finding out she was a lesbian. Besides, she did not want to end up in any tabloids. She was a virgin and allowed me to be the "first" to penetrate her. She technically lost her virginity with a strap- on penis. After six months, I was tired of being in a relationship. She had some emotional issues that I was too young to be sensitive enough to understand. It began to drain me when she cried about her problems.

The Lingo 101- Secret Society

I had just turned 19 feeling like I was the man making moves in the street with an arrogant attitude. It was my second Los Angeles Gay Pride at Zuma Beach, and now my hair was cut, which made a drastic change in my appearance. This gay boy approached me and handed me a flyer.

"You look real," he said.

I was not sure what he meant, but I assumed it was a compliment about my masculinity.

The flyer was for a competition called a **"ball."** This was an underground society within itself like an LGBT sorority. These two guys from the House of Diamante told me to come to Philadelphia and walk. A **"House"** is what the gay sororities are called. **"Walk"** is basically the term used for competing. Technically, you are walking down a runway. I did not attend that engagement, but I became highly interested in something new that was not happening in Los Angeles.

Shortly after hearing of these competitions, they were mentioned again. I met a guy named Red who was visiting Los Angeles. He admired my **"realness,"** (my ability to pass for the opposite sex). His friend asked where he could buy some ecstasy pills. I told him that I sold them.

"I thought you were a fine boy," he said.

We chuckled and had a great time that night at the club.

Red recruited me for his House. The name "ball" would lead you to think it was a formal event, but you could wear anything. He was the **"Father"** of the House of Essence, which was the position held by a masculine gay man in charge of the House. There was also a **"Mother"** who was a feminine gay boy referred to as **"Butch Queen."** Later, as time evolved in the **ballroom scene**, only transsexuals were the mothers, which are called **"Fem Queens."**

"The kids," is a term for gays in general, but also in reference to the members of the House. The mother and father, **"house parents"** are responsible for preparing the House "kids" for the balls. They make sure the house is running smoothly. They conduct meetings to inform the kids of the uniformed dress code concepts for the balls. We paid dues to purchase tables at the balls. The mother and father supervised rehearsals to critique some of the kids' performance. We voted other members in at the meetings also.

Red became my personal gay father who showed me the ropes in the ballroom scene. Many females did not resemble boys during that time, and he was eager for me to win trophies for his House. I became a member of the House of Essence walking a category called **"Butch Realness"** designed for girls who look like boys. Like anything else, there was a lot of ballroom politics. The judges threw "**shade,**" which means they acted catty towards us.

Our House was the underdogs in the ballroom arena in that era. Red had a lot of members who turned their category. "**Turned it**" meant you were exceptionally on point in your presentation or performance, also referred to as **"slayed."** The judges did not vote fairly, and other Houses that were established for longer periods of time would win the categories. Some of the other Houses were called: Miyake-Mugler, Givenchy, Ebony, Escada, Armani, Diamante, Latex, Extravaganza, Milan, Allure, Prada, Chanel, and Ninja. Most Houses were named after a fashion designer.

From the time we met, Red flew me out of state to walk my category. He bought me clothes and paid my way into these functions. I was underage, so he also got a fake ID made for me. Most of the balls were thrown at nightclubs where you had to be twenty-one. Eventually, people rented reception halls to avoid the age restrictions, and maximize selling liquor themselves. I realized that I could make extra money at the balls selling cocaine and ecstasy pills. It would also be advantageous for me to save money on my own habits.

As a teenager making over a thousand dollars on a weekend trip, seemed like tons of money. I would **"snatch"** (win) for my category. It was no denying my realness ability to pass for the opposite sex. My breasts were not visible, my haircuts were precise with sideburns, and my demeanor was boyish. I looked like a pretty boy opposed to a hard-ugly dude. I had pizazz and confidence that demanded the room's attention. I would wear my strap-on penis under my pants and grab my crotch at the judge's panel. The crowd would **"go up"** (cheer) with excitement.

A year after I was in the House of Essence, we merged with a more recognized House called Givenchy. After I was introduced to this underground society it became a lifestyle for a lifetime. Ballroom was an adrenaline rush to hit that runway. I attended these balls about twice a month flying from Los Angeles to major cities like Atlanta, New York, Philadelphia, and Washington, D.C. I frequented Atlanta the most, because they had huge turnouts and better establishments.

Everyone was aspiring to climb the ladder of notoriety in these gay pageants. There are levels of achievement called **"Stars, Statements, and Legends."** The ultimate goal, which took many years to achieve, was to reach the top status of a "Legend." For example, if you won or made an impact walking for a few years, they would call you out in the beginning as a "Star." "Statements" had a little more clout, and had about 5 years of winning under their belt. "Legends" were participants who had been in the ballroom scene for ten years or more with an outstanding track record of winning and making grand entrances. SSL's is an acronym for Stars, Statements, and Legends, which is a roll call before the ball started to publicly recognize them. More recently, the epitome of elevation was to be deemed an **"ICON."**

The way the balls operate is that you walk down the runway to a panel of an uneven number of judges. You had to get **"10's,"** which meant the approval to compete in the category. If one judge said **"chop"** by holding up a prop, you were disqualified. The phrase for being chopped was, "I don't see it." If you got your 10's you stood to the side. It was a process of elimination. Once all the opponents were given their 10's the commentator paired you off in twos for the judges to vote. The uneven number of judges breaks the tie if necessary.

The commentator, Eric Bizarre, was the **"fiercest"** – defined as the best on the mic in the late 90's. When they had dance categories called **"Vogue Fem,"** he would say, *"What's new miss pussycat feelin' a lil of this and that. The kitty cat cunt was past due for you have something new. Fred and Wilma and Barney too, let me see you vogue to my Yabba dabba doo. Pebbles, Pebbles, bam-bam."*

The competitors would drop to the floor into a dip on the "bam." Those nursery rhymes were called **"chants,"** which the commentator used to hype up the opponents to **"serve"** meaning make a good impression on the judges for their categories. "Vogueing" is popular in ballroom and it can take hours to get through that category. There are so many butch queens (gay boys) that vogue fem. They would express their femininity with costumes, wigs, and flamboyant hand gestures. Fem Queens (transsexuals) would have their separate categories to vogue fem too. A lot of shade (cattiness) was thrown between the kids. Everybody wanted to be **"cunty"** (feminine as possible) in their performance.

My father Red was "legendary" for **"Streetwear"** **(urban clothing)** and **"Realness with a Twist."** The category "Realness with a Twist" was entertaining in the aspect that the boys had to get their 10's for looking like they were not gay at all. Then they came back dressed feminine and vogued fem. They would show out in that category by tying up their shirts, wearing colorful wigs, and some would have on high heels. That category was what they called a **"kee kee"** meaning hilarious.

The **"face"** categories were a main attraction also competing for beauty. A term for a gorgeous person is **"sitting."** Those categories displayed the features of cheek bones, skin, nose, chin, and teeth. "Butch Queen Face" is for gay boys, and the "Fem Queen Face" is for transsexuals. "Butch Queen up in Drags Face" is for gay boys in drag that looked like a pretty woman. The real biological females walked "Women's face." Gay boys called women **"fish"** or **"lipstick lesbians."**

These face categories were exciting because they would have productions with props. The grand entrances would be **"rock socking"** meaning breath taking. I believe $10,000 was the largest grand prize in the face category. My tranny best friend, Cee Cee, won all the major grand prizes for the Fem Queen face. My friend Jay would always win for the Butch Queen face category. Jay was still in high school when they first recruited him to walk as an Ebony. As time progressed, he became a member of the House of Milan.

The body categories always got the kids all riled up, because they got naked. They called **"Sex Siren"** and **"Body."** They had to sell the illusion of sex and have a muscular physique. They would be greased down with tons of baby oil. The person who **"sold it"** (made their presence known the most) would snatch the trophy and cash. Usually, the one who revealed his/her private parts would win.

"Thug Realness," "Pretty Boy Realness," and "Schoolboy Realness" were categories for the butch queens (gay boys), and were really mind bogglers. "Thug Realness" was for dudes who did not look gay, but passed off for thugs. Some of these men are *"down low"* brothers with baby mamas. "Pretty Boy Realness" was designed for those who had handsome features, but they did not look feminine or gay. "Schoolboy Realness" was boys who could pass for being heterosexual at school.

Several of them who walked the realness categories were called **"bottoms"** meaning those who get penetrated. A **"top"** is the one who does the penetrating. **"Verse"** (shortened for versatile) meant you would flip flop and do either. A **"thot"** was a term for a whorish person – this seemed to be the actions of all those in the ballroom scene. Nobody had a sense of morals or integrity. The presentation of their looks was just an illusion like anybody in the circuit.

I had two friends, named Popper and B.D. that were in gangs on the streets of L.A. who walked thug realness. One was married with several kids, and the other one was single with children all over the place. They loved to travel to compete for thug realness. To their advantage, having gang tattoos, sagging pants, and a thuggish demeanor caused them to win. The three of us always won our realness category when we walked out of state. We never came back to Los Angeles defeated.

Years after I was involved in this underground society, they created a category for **"Transmen."** That was for those who were born as females, but began to take testosterone. They had surgeries to remove their breasts and got pec implants to display men's muscular chest. They grew beards and had very deep voices. Their clitoris grew like a child's penis from the hormones. I always was intrigued by friends in the ballroom scene who went this route. I was tempted, but my God-conscience would not let me begin the next phase. I was satisfied with my illusion and capability to pass for a male without the hormones. I knew how to flatten my breasts even making them invisible by wearing a tank top. I was unsure about how I would look with a beard, and I always had in the back of my mind "what if" I return to my upbringing and foundation of holiness.

Many transsexuals were good friends of mine. They used their penis to penetrate clients, and any other person who would allow them. All the boys who walked *"realness"* who dated transsexuals were labeled **"tranny chasers"** (men who date transsexuals). There were transmen/butches (studs) who had birthed children with transsexuals and gay men. In the "LGBTQ Ballroom community" anything seemed to be permissible. I made some rounds in this circle of perversion. For a season, I had a strong lust for tranny's. I also had a weakness for those that walked face. Two fem queens (transsexuals) dating was common. Everybody wanted to sleep with one another.

Perversion has no rules; whatever appeases your sexual appetite is what people lust after.

The fashion categories were popular because the contenders were able to flaunt their **"pieces"** (clothing). There was a category called **"best-dressed spectator"** meaning you were not walking the ball, but you came **"totally done"** in costly apparel from head to toe. The **"Foot and Eyewear"** category required a **"sickening"** (exceptionally nice, extravagant) expensive pair of frames, with a **"nasty"** (striking) pair of heels or men's dress shoes/boots.

The kids came out to "slay" for the **"Labels"** category. That is to say, to make a show-stopping impression. The entire ensemble including your underwear, socks, and accessories were designer pieces. The kids say, "That outfit is everything. You ate it, Miss Thing." These fashion categories gave thousands of dollars away because people spent money to prepare for them. Truth be told, most of the kids were what we called **"stunt queens"** (criminals who write bogus checks or use other people's stolen credit profiles to order these items). The merchandise was sent out by FedEx to empty apartments or P.O. boxes.

The ballroom had categories for every gender – even catering to overweight people. It was called **"Big Boys"** Face, European Runway, Labels, Vogueing etc. and there were **"Big Girls"** categories too. I guess it was considered unfair for those who were heavyset to have to compete against those smaller in stature. They took their categories seriously, and would have this attitude on the runway of such assurance that you had to let them live. The commentator would say, **"You better emote girl!"** which means to portray emotion in a theatrical manner. **"Unbothered"** is a term for not worried about anyone's opinion of you. The big girls sure had that attitude just like the others.

The majority of gay people in these "Houses" are either prostitutes or con artists. Nobody works a legit job. The transsexuals make their money on a website called Erosguide.com. The gay boys post on several sites like:

Rentboy, Men4rent, and Backpage.com. Most ballroom kids; live with each other or in hotels, abuse drugs, and make careers out of prostitution. They market sex as "massages with a happy ending" on the internet.

Everyone is seeking the approval of others in this society. The measures of desperation that people take is ludicrous to be recognized amongst a bunch of shady characters. A lot of people are not close with their biological families, they are ostracized behind their sexuality, and homeless. They feel like Houses are families within itself. The core of it all is phony. As soon as someone walked off the gays would **"read"** them (talk bad about them).

There were classifications of "the kids" even in the ballroom scene. Everyone was referred to as **"Miss, Honey, Miss Thing, or Girl."** If you made a sarcastic remark that was referred to as **"trying it."** They always called me Miss Esko. They did not care if you looked like a dude or even a man walking thug realness, to the kids you were still "Miss." Everything was referred to in the feminine form. Even the days of the week were referred to as "she." If they were waiting on the weekend one would say, "I cannot wait until she gets here, Miss Friday can't get here fast enough."

Those who were unpopular, unattractive, and without a craft (hustle) were called **"late and tired."** Those who were popular, attractive, dressed **fab** (fabulous), and had confidence were called, **"beat."** All of those who fit the criteria for "beat" were referred to as one of **"the girls."** The phrase "the girls" were an elite group who used the expression, **"You can't sit with us."** If you didn't fit in with the pretty people, they threw you shade (acted indifferent). **"What's the wave?"** meant, what are the plans for the night. **"Tea"** meant gossip or what's up. Suppose someone said, "I got some hot tea" that meant gossip. If they asked, "What's tea?" That meant what's up.

I became known for starting a trend using "tea" after the last word in a sentence. For example, I would say, "I cannot wait to party tonight tea." I called everybody by the name Annie. They started saying that as well in the urban LGBT scene. That was like a warm greeting I said to everyone, "What's tea, Annie?" I had a refreshing personality that liked to joke and party all the time. People started calling everyone "Linda" as a universal name too. The lingo continually evolves in the LGBT urban culture.

I always was in the well-known circle from the beginning. I was one of "the girls" due to, my gay father was a Legend, I was his son, always dressed in the latest streetwear, and sold drugs. Homosexual men referred to as "the kids" loved my personality, and the feelings were mutual. I began to hang around all gay boys much of the time.

I always said the gays have a place for anyone to fit in. Whether you're obese, tall, skinny, dark, light or white they will validate whomever into the LGBT community.

You never knew anyone's legal name regardless of the years of history shared. Everyone used a nickname. Most gay people are so vindictive and untrustworthy it was wise to stay mysterious to prevent a **"jaded girl"** (jealous homosexual) from turning you in to the police. In the past, people have given the police incriminating information about other homosexuals. In some instances, to stop an opponent from attending the ball, plane tickets were reported as fraudulent. That is what's called a **"shade fest."** The kids would say, "Somebody got her together she got locked" (snitched on and put in jail). They are so **"catty"** (maliciously sarcastic).

The urban LGBT community is a large disloyal group of opportunists. If I can just keep it 100, no one's loyalty lies anywhere. If opportunity knocks they are taking it. The main percentage of fights were caused by somebody sleeping with a friend's **"piece"** (lover). Everyone wanted to seem relevant, so the competition and jealousy were tense. Ballroom created a lot of enemies. Having two people walk the same category became a conflict of interest.

In a sense, it was like a "gay gang." Houses created rivals and huge fights transpired between them. People have been brutally beaten, stabbed, run over by cars – and as time progressed there have been victims of shootings.

Other Houses evolved from Ebony, Mugler, and Allure named Prodigy, Balenciaga, and St. Laurent. That caused tension and was possibly the reason some of the large fights occurred.

God's Word says:

Furthermore, just as they did not think it worthwhile to retain the knowledge of God, so God gave them over to a depraved mind, so that they do what ought not to be done. They have become filled with every kind of wickedness, evil, greed and depravity. They are full of envy, murder, strife, deceit and malice. They are gossips, slanderers, God-haters, insolent, arrogant and boastful; they invent ways of doing evil; they disobey their parents; they have no understanding, no fidelity, no love, no mercy. Although they know God's righteous decree that those who do such things deserve death, they not only continue to do these very things but also approve of those who practice them. Romans 1:28-32 (NIV)

Balls were not being held in California until maybe, the year 2000. I was the first person to establish a relevant House Chapter in Los Angeles, which was called Givenchy. I was promoted to the position of "father" of the house. There were two Houses in Los Angeles prior called Rodeo' and Ferragamo that did not travel to ballroom capitals. Personally, as Esko Givenchy, I threw the 3rd ball in Los Angeles, and was also the first commentator on the West Coast. Los Angeles was not yet recognized as a ballroom city. We had to create our own ballroom scene to gain respect and spark the interest of others to come from out of town. I was still travelling to walk "butch realness."

The two founders of the House of Givenchy, Zandy and Zack fell out. The house split up, and the overall "father" Zandy started the House of Mizrahi, so everyone including myself transitioned with him. Zandy has been wearing blonde hair as his trademark since I can remember. After about a year's time, he and Mother Zack reconciled their differences and reunited. Zack was also a commentator that was very innovative on the mic. The fiercest commentator Eric Bizarre, had passed away. This was a very sad era in the ballroom community.

A lot of people in the ballroom scene have died, which greatly impacted the community. Drug abuse, drunk driving fatalities, and unprotected sex caused the demise of many. Half of those in the ballroom community have been infected with HIV. The non-profit organizations would go over the statistics during the intermission at the balls. They tested many of the ballroom kids in exchange for gift cards or free tickets to the ball. These organizations began to sponsor the balls as the years went by to bring HIV awareness to the community.

People frequently went to jail flying on illegitimate arrangements. I was instructed to say a family member sent for me to attend a reunion and I'm not sure which one. Well, the time had come to utilize this alibi. One day, I was **"pooched"** meaning looking good and feeling proud in first class. The plane was scheduled to depart shortly. Two men in suits approached me at my seat.
"Step off the aircraft."
My heart dropped, I just knew they were going to **"clamp me"** (arrest).
"You better make other arrangements because the payment was declined," the airport policemen said.
"Oh, my gosh. I flew in for a family reunion. One of my relatives made the arrangements. I will get this straightened out," I said, politely.
"Alrighty, your things will be waiting for you in Los Angeles," he said.

I called a ride and got out of that airport as fast as I could. I was annoyed that my luggage was on the plane headed to Los Angeles, but my freedom was more important. I was stuck in Atlanta an extra day and had to fly out through another carrier.

TESTIMONY
I went to Detroit, Michigan for a ball. Someone forgot to pack socks so we ran to Wal Mart. As we approached the store entrance, two people were in

front of the store with a stand set up for donations. I usually noticed the Salvation Army ringing a bell with a bucket in front of stores. This was an extraordinary encounter, which I believe were angels. There were two middle aged Black women in all white with a sign that read, "Apostolic Missionaries." How ironic it was to see people representing the denomination I was raised under. *"Some people have shown hospitality to angels without knowing it"* (Hebrews 13:2 NIV). As quick as we grabbed the socks and came out, in less than ten minutes, they were gone. It was no sight of their sign or presence anywhere. That baffled me to no end, and I knew the Lord was using them to get my attention. I never mentioned it to the gay people who accompanied me, but as soon as I was alone, I called to tell my mom.

If you think about it, the devil has designed this dark underground path of homosexuality to pervert the God-given talents of many. God calls Christians "His children." The Enemy has homosexuals calling themselves "the kids." Whose kids? The devil's.

The bible describes:
"You belong to your father, the devil, and you want to carry out your father's desires. He was a murderer from the beginning, not holding to the truth, for there is no truth in him. When he lies, he speaks his native language, for he is a liar and the father of lies" (John 8:44 NIV).

Christians have adopted these gay lingo phrases not realizing that words carry spirits.

The Bible says life and death are in the power of the tongue. Utilizing terms derived from a perverse culture opens the door for evil spirits to enter your life.

The LGBT "ballroom arena" is the darkest realm you could enter in the homosexual lifestyle.

'Ballroom' becomes more than a hobby, it consumes you. It is a FALSE sense of stardom making people attempt to uphold an image they created in their mind. People participate in this activity for a living by traveling to compete in different states and posting prostitution ads. The pride, deceit, malice, gossip, and scandals are all designed to tear one another down. Only the strong survive. I never witnessed so much drama and friendships destroyed until I was introduced to this underground society. Older gay men prey on the younger to recruit them and ruin their lives before it starts.

Held Hostage

Every year I traveled to Atlanta, in January for Martin Luther King weekend and in September for Gay Pride during Labor Day. My gay father, Red arranged flights for all the "House Members" to come and stay with him. He was a black-market travel agent flying people anywhere for half price. He made reservations over the phone paying with stolen credit card information. There was always a major ballroom competition during these holiday weekends. We would have so much fun being up all night at his house. Red always rented an SUV for all of us to pile up in. He stayed down the street from Piedmont Park, which was a landmark for gay men to randomly have sex in the woods.

I blended right in with the boys as we walked to the park after midnight. I never knew that gay males had so many opportunities for casual sex. I literally witnessed them engage in sex with no exchanging of conversation at all. It was merely eye contact that these advances were made. I always wore my strap-on penis in a harness attached to my body. I joined in with the group on a guy bent over against a tree. The guy was so high sniffing vapors in a bottle called "poppers," he did not know who was behind him taking turns.

Perversion can take you into some dark dimensions of sexual promiscuity. I was fixated on utilizing my strap-on penis, which made me feel like a man. It was a mental hang-up that caused me to adopt this plastic penis as a part of my identity. I received pleasure from the pressure of the suction cup against my private part.

Sin opened the door to all kinds of things, going along with the environment at the moment.

This night was festive at Red's house preparing for the club. I was already dressed and waiting on others who were getting ready. The music was loud. We heard a pounding steady knock at the door. Someone lowered the volume of the stereo. Red came down and answered the door. Two men invited themselves in. You could tell by their demeanor they were upset. None of the guests had any idea who these men were, but Red seemed to be familiar with them. Without hesitation, they drew guns and confronted Red concerning some business deal that went sour. These men had heavy Jamaican accents.

"Our cousin has been put in jail on the plane ticket you sold man," they said, fussing.

Apparently, the credit card was reported stolen, and the person flying got arrested.

"Hey, y'all listen up, this townhouse is surrounded by five men outside. You better not make any moves," one of the men announced.

"As a punishment, you will be shot in the foot," the other man said, demanding a refund and forcing him upstairs.

We were all terrified, but hesitant to flee out the sliding door because they said the place was surrounded. One man came downstairs and took our money and jewelry too. I felt like this was about to end in a massacre. I began praying under my breath.

"Jesus, Jesus, Jesus," I kept saying.

"It was a mistake. My apologies guys, I can bail him out on Monday," Red said, from upstairs pleading for mercy.

All of us visiting were from various states looking at one another terrified like, 'What have we gotten entangled in?' The chaos was in motion for about 30 minutes. Suddenly, we heard another knock at the door. Our eyes got big as my heart raced. I was wondering if it was the men surrounding the house. Red was escorted by one gentleman with the gun to the door. When Red swung the door open it was the police.

"Hi, we received a complaint of an altercation," the officer said.

"Oh, no officer, everything is okay," Red replied, nervously.

Everyone leaped up at that moment behind Red motioning to the police officer for help.

"You two gentlemen step outside," the officer said to Red and the robber whose gun was tucked away.

"Hey, the neighbor called in a disturbance here," the other officer stated, as he stepped inside.

My friend revealed that we were being robbed and the other armed man was hiding upstairs. The police summoned him down with his gun drawn. The man surrendered without any resistance. The two Jamaican men were arrested and our properties were retrieved. The five other people were never present outside. The Jamaicans lied using that as a clever fear tactic.

That incident was a clear indication we should have remained still for the night. I was grateful, embracing the reality of our protection and the intervention of God. Psalm 91:11(NIV) says, *"For he will command his angels concerning you to guard you in all your ways."* We were so blessed to have escaped the brunt of that episode. After all of that, we still went out.

It amazes me how nothing stops you when you're under the devil's influence.

The first gay guy that I met named Ramone in Los Angeles had moved to Atlanta. I was so glad to run into him at the club. It would be the last time I saw him. He passed away months later. His body was flown back to Los Angeles. That funeral was like a gay reunion. I saw my ex Courtney the actress, and a host of others I remembered from when I first hit the gay scene.

Gremlins

One fourth of July weekend, some acquaintances from other states came to Los Angeles for Gay Pride. I was a well-established drug dealer with meth, cocaine, ecstasy, and marijuana with a large clientele. My apartment was a frequent hangout for gay people to get high. I knew these two individuals from the Atlanta ballroom scene. They both had enormous cocaine habits. I made hundreds of dollars a day from them alone.

Their names in the ballroom scene were Asia Allure and AC Chanel. Asia was a tranny and AC was a gay boy. They were both on check writing sprees on Rodeo' Drive in Beverly Hills. They were getting thousands of dollars in merchandise and altering the receipts to get cash returns to bypass the 7-day clearance policy. These two criminals did not use good judgment being greedy. Luckily, they did not get arrested, but their money came to a halt.

Initially, they had a rental car and now they were not able to pay for it. The checks were reported fraudulent in the system. They could not pay for their hotel room anymore either. They asked to stay at my house for about a week to hustle their airfare to get back home. I agreed. We began to club nightly. Afterward, we would hang in Leimert Park, the 'gay cruising area.' They started putting the cocaine in their cigarettes and swiveling out some of the tobacco. I was not comfortable with them smoking primos in my presence. I was not going to allow them to take me back down that road.

Their patterns became unproductive as they overindulged in drugs. Smoking cigarettes laced with cocaine inside my house created a 'loud' odor. I became paranoid that my neighbors would think I was smoking crack. They left cigarette butts all over my house from ripping the tips off to get a stronger puff. They slept all day and woke up in the late afternoon. They were very sloppy housekeepers.

Their one week stay flew by. All the money they got was spent with me on their drug habits, so they had no resources to vacate. I did not know them that well. I was barely able to sleep with them there. I was thinking they might find my stash of drugs or money and vanish. I should have been focused on their departure, but instead, my own greed preferred their patronage. Their presence was so exhausting that I could barely think with clarity. I had the responsibility of being the "father" of the House of Givenchy, which required extra funds. I was under a lot of pressure to maintain a House reputation of excellent presentation in my region. Also, I was obligated to recruit others to travel for the 'balls.'

I was using drugs and not relying on my better judgment. It took a month of their squatting to make me overwhelmed with their company. I felt like I had no privacy and my house was a mess. I liked a clean home and when I was high, I compulsively cleaned up a lot. They were like having two children around. I became annoyed at cleaning more than usual. Eventually, I let my house remain filthy with tobacco on the carpet, clothes scattered, and ashtrays full of cigarettes.

My mental health became compromised due to the lack of sleep and a cluttered setting. I started to get extremely frustrated, wondering how I got myself in this predicament. These opportunists had really taken advantage of my kindness. I did a pretty good job keeping up a tough image on the streets, but those who knew me personally were cognizant of my huge heart. I believe my upbringing instilled the love of God, so I constantly helped people.

Finally, after 3 months of having these guests that my mom called the "gremlins," they flew back home. I was very delirious from short intervals of sleep. Months of inadequate rest was taking its toll on me. I was mentally disoriented and could not get to my parents' house fast enough to regroup. I pulled my car into their driveway and placed a car cover on it.

I Tried

I was really gaining my foothold at my parents' house as I rested. I spent days sleeping, eating, and lying in bed. My play Aunt Anna, a dear friend to my mother had stopped by. I was back in my room watching television, and my mom asked me to come out and greet her. Before she left, we gathered in a circle to pray. I remember feeling the presence of God in our living room. I felt like I needed a break from my vicious pattern of unproductivity. The strongholds of battling addiction and my sexuality were caving in on me. I felt the love of God as tears rolled down my face. An invisible embrace seemed to be cradling me.

Aunt Anna asked if I wanted to go to Monday night prayer. It was starting in about an hour, and I agreed to go. I felt so broken and taken advantage of by people who constantly preyed on my kindness. The gay community was full of leeches – the guests who finally left had taken me through the ringer. I was in search of the peace that escaped my life years ago. I never even contemplated why I was being drawn back toward the Lord. I just went with the leading of the Holy Spirit knowing that God would not hurt me.

Once we entered, it was quiet in the sanctuary with people scattered throughout on their knees praying. The lights were so dim, you could not see many faces, only silhouettes. I went and kneeled at the altar and began to ask God to forgive me for my life's detour. I burst out crying and speaking in tongues. I felt like every burden I had bottled up had been given to the Lord. Weights were lifted off me, and I was as light as a feather. I knew my life needed a change for the better. It was the year of 2002, which was referred to as the millennium. I was deciding to go back to my first love Jesus Christ.

I was no longer going to the barber, and I got my hair braided into some individual extensions to help it grow. I had no long-term plans for my future and just wanted to seek inner consolation. I felt I was ready to try reverting to my Pentecostal roots. I had a heart of compassion and wanted others to make it to heaven. My cousin Calvin had already spread his wings away from our holy upbringing. I was coming back to Christ, while he was establishing a new life down the dark road of Hollywood's entertainment industry.

I began to call up some of my female friends who I referred to as sisters in the gay lifestyle to share the gospel with them. They were glad to hear from me after my disappearing act left everyone clueless. I wanted to share with all of them that I loved what God was beginning to do in my life. As a duty to prevent being responsible for their souls, I was eager to tell people Jesus saves. The decision was theirs to make concerning Acts 2:38 salvation.

More friends than I expected took me up on the invitation to church. My close gay male friend Ashton visited church one Sunday to see me. He was supportive of my transition, but a little surprised I was in women's apparel. Afterward he came over for dinner. We had been friends for about 7 years since he moved to California from Detroit. He always had my back and was ready to fight anyone who had an issue with me. I was glad to see him, and we kept in touch.

My two lesbian friends Keisha and Natasha came to visit my church with their children shortly after Ashton. They were really touched by the message and cried during the altar call. Paralyzed by fear, they did not get up to walk down the aisle, but I knew the Lord was drawing them. We sat in the pew after the dismissal of the service meditating on the message.

Natasha said she was ready for a change, but tormented with alcoholism. The thought of getting my friend Rocky that was her live-in girlfriend out of the apartment seemed overwhelming to her. I told her she was thinking too far ahead and whatever God's plan was for her life, He would lead the way.

Keisha was struggling with homosexuality and her bad habits. I tried assuring her that waiting until she felt she could stop was a trick of the "enemy" to keep her bound. I did not pressure anyone to get baptized. I was just glad at the mere fact that they showed up.

I started looking for a job because I was no longer going to be making money illegally. My parents bought me a black, women's pantsuit to wear to interviews. My work experience was minimal, so it was challenging getting back into the swing of things. I went to a non-profit community center to take some computer and job training courses. Rising early in the morning was certainly a new adjustment. I was getting accustomed to a normal sleep schedule and responsibility as an adult. However, I felt a tad bit forced and obligated to my parents. I knew automatically from my religious church upbringing that my men's dress attire was against protocol.

I was going through the motions as I made the attempt to change the outward appearance. As I reflect, I realize the intent of my heart was not desperate for deliverance. I looked the part, but the process never fully cultivated. I was more interested in making my parents proud of me. They were now remarried. My father's drill sergeant antics were not as bad, but he still had that sense of control that spilled over into my adulthood. On one or two occasions, Dad would toss cold water into the shower as he did when I was growing up. Despite his personality quirks, I loved my dad for raising me and supporting me through life.

After completing the eight-week job training course, I was hired at a telemarketing company. I was responsible for calling random businesses to sell them printer cartridges. That did not go so well as all I encountered were dial tones. Several people would hang up as soon as they heard my introduction. After a month, they let me go because my sales margin never escalated.

I attempted to find odd jobs in the paper like selling knives door to door but that seemed potentially dangerous. I got hired up on Wilshire Blvd. in a high-rise building making more cold calls. This was a different type of telemarketing completing surveys about movies. I did alright for a few months, but they had a status quota and monitored the calls. I had been warned once about being sarcastic with the customers. Then I was written up for arguing with someone who was rude to me. Once I returned from a suspension, my final check was waiting for me in the office.

Not being able to find stable employment was discouraging. I really was not satisfied reconnecting with the ministry either. The church was certainly a soul saving station. They baptized in the name of Jesus on the spot anytime someone wanted to be saved. I was already saved, so I was bored at my home church feeling like I was not receiving enough prophetic impartation. I knew that I had spiritual gifts, but they were not developed because the pastor was not one who operated in prophecy, miracles, healing etc.

The people at the church were stuck in tradition. Stockings were mandatory for women, and neckties for men. Although they were dressed up, their spirits were offensive and many did not show love – walking past one another grudgingly. People go through all types of things to get to church, but when you get there you don't feel adequate to be there. The older women would hunt down the younger ladies with stockings that they kept in their cars. A self-righteous spirit resided there, and encouragement was scarce. Some of the saints were critical with no discernment.

I was sincerely trying to transition. I re-enrolled in Bible College and was given a scholarship by the school for my tuition. My driver's license was suspended, which probably was a good thing to keep me settled while being spiritually grounded. One of the church members ended up paying off my traffic tickets to reinstate my license. Although she meant well, it was too premature in my spiritual walk. I started visiting my play sister Natasha's house who attended the same church. My good friend Rocky was in a relationship with her living at her house.

I knew the church left a good impression on my two friends Keisha and Natasha because they came back. Ultimately, they got baptized in the name of Jesus and received the Holy Ghost speaking with other tongues. Their two young sons were the same age, and liked the church. I was so happy now that some friends from my past had been converted. I felt like we were all in this together now.

I recall going to a service with my Aunt Lona hearing Dr. Jacquelyn McCullough preach. The late Bishop Robert McMurray was still alive and hosted the service. This evangelist preached on "The Backslider." She talked about the story of the prodigal son. I never imagined that the things she spoke of would be experienced later. I never forgot that message after the day she preached it.

My pastor's wife, who had invested so much time and finances in me as a child/teenager, had been very sick. She was the reason I initially left the church because of her mistreatment. I had truly forgiven her and considered that incident to be water under the bridge. On Mother's Day Sunday, the first lady died. Before we left home, our phone rang with the sad news. My mom was hysterically crying and pacing the floor. I was crushed in disbelief, not aware of the severity of her illness. She was like another mother in a sense, and had a nurturing side. The Lord called her home to be with Him. That was the saddest Sunday morning service at the church. A lot of saints were in the parking lot crying.

I finished out the semester at Bible College. I was struggling with going forward and reverting backward. Keisha and Natasha continued to attend church and their two sons both eight years old got baptized and filled with the Holy Spirit. They never stopped clubbing, drinking, smoking etc., but it was not my place to judge. One of my ex-girlfriends came into the picture when Natasha invited her to church. Her name was Nancy, and she was saved at my church too.

Keisha invited some other lesbians who were two biological sisters, and they got saved. Afterward, my other stud friend 'S' (Samantha) who was really close to me attended church on Sunday nights. She was filled with the Holy Ghost when my mom laid hands on her at the altar. Samantha was reluctant to get baptized, but she did it once we explained the importance of being immersed in JESUS name. God was dealing with her heavily at that time, and she had already stopped wearing men's clothes. I was amazed at what God was doing in this six-month time frame. A whirlwind of His spirit swept through my circle of friends. I felt so excited about all these young ladies that had been born again. We all were attending bible study on Wednesday nights too.

I began visiting my play sister Natasha's house a lot as an outlet away from home. She was attempting her new walk with Christ, but her body was apparently going through withdrawals. My old buddy Rocky voluntarily bought her some cold beer from the corner store. I believe that was a tactic to enable her. Rocky wanted to keep her intoxicated to salvage their relationship. That really was not the best environment for me to be in as I adapted to change.

After a while, on a hot summer day, I found myself having a cold beer with Natasha. Using alcohol led to the desire to smoke a cigarette. I felt condemned about being a follower instead of standing firm on sobriety like a leader. I can understand why the Bible instructs us to *stay away from every kind of evil* (1 Thessalonians 5:22 NLT). My 6-month sobriety mark had now been broken. I had a few beers and smoked a few cigarettes to escape the sorrow over the death of the first lady. I had truly shared more great memories than bad with her.

My pastor got remarried two months after the first lady died. He told everyone in an introduction to his sermon that the Lord instructed him to do this. It was a split in emotions, some understood while others disapproved. Nonetheless, I felt like our pastor did not take enough time to mourn or allow the church to grieve. I left it in God's hands because it was not a sin to remarry, but it affected some people.

Natasha, being a new member was in disbelief and stopped attending altogether. Keisha was in agreement with the marriage, giving the pastor the benefit of a doubt. I ended up falling into sin with my ex-girlfriend Nancy who was coming to church. That soul tie was never broken between us. It was not wise for us to reconnect trying to be friends after a history of intimacy. Nancy took me back into the web of unnatural lust. Because of talking to Ashton, informing me on the latest news my flesh became enticed. Also hanging out with my play sister who was not delivered was a hindrance.

A few beers and cigarettes led me right back to accepting an invitation to a party. My friend B.D. of many years that was truly like a brother was coming home from prison. I thought since some old friends rented a reception hall, and it was not being hosted at a club, that it would be okay. He used to stay with me for a while before he got locked up. He was a "*down low*" gang member who was active in the LGBT ballroom society. I missed church that Sunday evolving into character for the festivities. I would have been embarrassed to go around my old peers dressed feminine. My other play brother Popper took me to get my hair braided straight back in cornrows, and a barber lined it across the front. He bought me a men's Raiders football hoodie, some black Levis jeans, and a pair of Jordan's.

I was a little socially removed at the party standing in a corner all night. I felt out of place. Initially, I tried to remain inconspicuous. My friend B.D. was happy to see me. I had one too many strong cocktails and loosened up by the middle of the night. Some people didn't recognize me right away. I had picked up about fifteen pounds sober off narcotics, and my head was no longer bald.

From that night forward, I decided to start building the things I once destroyed. Something was telling me I was too young to live such a reserved lifestyle for Christ. I can admit that was the devil in my ear, and I thought Christianity was to be lived by the elderly. This decision to have one last hoorah turned into more dramatic encounters than my first ten years could fathom. I can relate to the scripture that says *a backslider takes on seven more demons*. If I could have seen my future, I would have stayed sweetly saved under the ark of safety.

"There is a way that appears to be right, but in the end, it leads to death" (Proverbs 14:12, NLT).

I was baited back into debauchery. My Mom was in complete utter shock that it appeared my progression was accelerating, but I suddenly shifted into reverse. She cornered me with a butcher knife and screamed, "Damn girl! Are you insane?" I bolted out of the kitchen side door. She scared me with that outburst. My evangelist mother temporarily lost her composure. My dad was saved now, remarried to my mom, and they both were ganging up on me. I had a curfew that was impossible to keep if I wanted to go clubbing. My Dad put the chain on the door after 1:30 a.m. This reminded me of how as a kid he would lock us out coming from church. The club was not over until 2:00 a.m. so I certainly was not going to leave early in compliance with my parent's rules.

Sleeping with the Enemy

I left my parents' house and moved back to my low-income apartment to live my wild life in 2003. I was in the heart of the city where driving in a car, I could reach any central point in ten minutes. Hollywood was north, Inglewood toward the south, the extreme ghetto was east, and the beach in the west. I could see the busy strip of Crenshaw from my window where low riders cruised on Sunday evenings. One of the largest parades for Martin Luther King was held on Crenshaw Blvd. every year.

One afternoon, I was taking the trash out and a woman recognized me while driving down my block.

"ESKO!" she yelled. Immediately, she pulled over, but I did not recognize the vehicle so I walked over to the truck.

"Um, hello," I said.

"Hey, do you remember me?" she asked.

"Not really," I said.

"We met at the after-hours club called 'Hole in the Wall.' I'm Candy Snow. We were at the bar talking and my girlfriend walked up rudely interrupting," she said.

"Oh, yeah, I recall that incident," I laughed.

"Hop in," she said.

She was driving a customized truck with gold spoke rims, suede seats, and marble swirl interior panels. I was shocked to see her randomly cruising down my residential street. I conversed with her for about thirty minutes or so. I was captivated with her beauty and yellow skin complexion, which I preferred. She made an impression on me with her seductive body language and intellectual conversation.

"With persuasive words, she led him astray; she seduced him with her smooth talk." Proverbs 7:21 (NIV)

She asked me if I bumped (a term for sniffing cocaine) as she simultaneously pulled out a small bag of cocaine filled to the top. I took a sniff in each nostril through a straw. My system was 7 months clean, so the first sniff was an instant freeze making my nose tingle and my senses alert.

"Do you have a job?" she asked.

"I just got out of jail, and I am trying to get back on my feet. I was a drug dealer before I had to do my time," I said.

Of course, I was lying about jail, but I was trying to sound hard core. It would have sounded corny to tell her for six months I was going to church trying to live holy. Candy volunteered to buy me some cocaine to re-establish my hustle.

Candy Snow had put her superhero cape on to rescue me. She purchased me a new phone, new clothes, and tennis shoes. She was twelve years older than me and more mature mentally. She used a lot of quick slick street talk like a crooked car salesman. She was one of those older women who dressed youthful and preyed on much younger companions to vicariously live through. Everyone appears to have good intentions in the beginning. It took me almost a decade to figure out who she really was. As you keep reading, it will make sense after a while.

Initially, Candy was tons of fun to creep around with. She still had ties with the same stud who interrupted us in the after-hours. They were married, but her wife had relapsed on crack. One night, Candy came over and talked my ear off with all her issues as we got high on cocaine and drank liquor. Candy said she had no idea her wife was a recovering addict. Hennessy had a half-sister named Cannon that was also a stud. She broke the news to Candy that Hennessy was on drugs again. Looking back now, once I got to know Candy much better I see why the wife got back on drugs.

Behind Enemy Lines

In the beginning, Candy and I had no sexual interaction. She would buy drugs and always seemed to be in a rush. Occasionally, she sat around with me and hung out at my house. I had my share of sex partners so it made no difference if we were not physical right away. My friend Rocky was calling me "scary" asking when I was going to make my move. I just ignored her, and was fine with the generosity Candy had shown thus far. Candy's material benefits and buying cocaine from me not expecting a handout was sufficient.

After four months, Candy had finally become intimate with me. She came over this night around ten with a bottle of alcohol venting about her girlfriend's disappearance for a month. I was planning to go out clubbing, but it was apparent the night was heading in another direction. I guess being a shoulder to cry on paid off with my patience to pursue the bedroom. She stayed the night and just like the movies, I woke up to an empty bed with a note beside it.

Candy and I began to see each other more often. We never interacted outside of my house. Eventually, she seemed to get a little clingy desiring more of my attention. My neighbors were not nosy so visitors to my house all day and night were not a concern. She started familiarizing herself with my circle gaining the approval of those whose opinion I valued. Everyone just loved Candy because she could hold a conversation about practically anything.

My mom and dad were divorcing for the second time, and she was going to have to move into my one-bedroom apartment. She was downsizing from their house to my place so there was only so much she could bring. I got rid of my furniture so that my mom could bring her things. That way my apartment would look like a home as opposed to a hangout. The apartment was a little crammed with both of our things combined.

The lease Candy and her wife shared ended. Her spouse was so far gone on crack, she never returned anyway. Candy asked me to be in a relationship with her, and I agreed. We began looking for a place together. Later, I found out she took care of her elderly father. She also had a teenage daughter and a son who was in college. Her son lived in another city playing college football. Her dad and daughter were residing elsewhere the entire time she lived a separate life with Hennessy. Now we would merge together, and find a three bedroom to accommodate everyone.

Mom was blessed to have my apartment for herself while I jumped the broom with Candy Snow. I packed up my clothes and moved out to have a sense of freedom without our lifestyles colliding. My mom was an evangelist, and I was a transgender, drug dealer, running with gang members. I felt it was for the best to allow my mom a sense of peace if I moved out. I did stop by weekly to say hello and check my mail.

Candy and I started to go to the balls (gay sorority pageants) together, which was all new to her. She was jealous of transsexuals because they looked better than she did. She made rude insulting comments about gay men as if she was not a lesbian. It was offensive because these were long term friends of mine before I crossed paths with her. She tried to make her comments seem like jokes, but they were malicious. Moreover, she started trying to tell me how to conduct my drug business with customers. I was starting to see the nitpicking side of Candy.

I finally introduced Candy to my mom after about six months. My mom was never going to embrace her as an extension of our family, but she was curious to know who I was living with. As a woman of God, my mom treated everyone kindly. Candy did not seem nervous and tried to act like my mom was an old friend of hers.
"Hey, how are you? I am Candy Snow," she said.
"Hello, I am blessed Candy. I am Ms. Rivers," mom said.

They were only ten years apart in age. However, anyone with etiquette would not introduce themselves by an alias name. This first visit was difficult being in the room with both of them. I never brought any woman I dated around my mom. I never lived with a woman either. I always played the field.

My mom asked Candy if she had any church background. Candy and I had never discussed religion, so I had no clue what Candy's answer would be. Candy responded that she was resentful toward God for allowing her virginity to be taken by being gang raped in ninth grade, as she walked home from school. She told us in detail about the Randy's Donut landmark on Normandie and Century. She said while waiting to order food in the line, she was abducted from behind in broad daylight. An unknown man snatched her and forced her into a garage in the apartments next door. Five or six men violated every hole in her body on a used box spring mattress puncturing her back, and they urinated on her. After an evening of abuse, she was released into the night hours walking home in a trance. To make matters worse, Candy said she contracted an STD, and was pregnant. Her older sister had a hysterectomy because of ovarian cancer, convinced her to keep the baby, and let her raise him. Then to top it off, she said her dad murdered some of the predators too.

Can you imagine hearing this traumatic story for the first time as you are sitting with your mother? I was thinking, my goodness! Who could survive such an awful incident. We were crying as she told this story. It made me question God about the bad hand she was dealt. It certainly made my mom compassionate toward her and reiterate God's unfailing love. I was not expecting our first visit to go this way. My mom got the oil and laid hands on Candy's forehead praying for her. I nicknamed Mom a "Holy Ghost gangster" because she rises to the occasion in boldness.

From that day forward, once Candy told that story, everything she said was outlandish. If anyone said something about themselves, she could tell a story that made their encounter sound minor. I started to think she was entering a creative writing contest. Most of our relationship was spent high on cocaine.

Candy reflected on old horrific stories, which made me fearful of her. She said she had been to prison before, and her husband was a hitman. They had been separated for years, but never divorced. She said he drove a man to the desert and made her murder a guy to prove her loyalty to the marriage. She also told me that she collected insurance checks on five out of nine dead ex-boyfriends during the marriage. There was so much other stuff, I can't even remember it all in that seven-year time span. I was getting annoyed with her after about a year and a half, and feeling regretfully overwhelmed. Candy was dramatic, controlling, and mentally unstable.

I start noticing how huge of an intake she had with cocaine. When I went to buy mine, she wanted two eight-balls on the side for herself. In a relationship, Candy was no longer able to conceal a lot of things. She was a great actor when we casually dated. Now, I discovered she really had no friends and was attached to me like a pet puppy. She preferred to stay secluded, high in a utopia, and have sex for a hobby. Now I realized why she liked dating younger people for constant sexual gratification.

She was a master manipulator. A person her own age would have seen right through her shenanigans. She turned into a bossy mother figure who was no longer fun being around. I was losing physical attraction for her. I started to see her vindictive side. It was challenging to disconnect because she kept me on such an emotional rollercoaster. Two women together are a "ticking time bomb" waiting to explode. It is too much estrogen. Women are caring creatures longing for love, and when they think they have discovered it they refuse to let go.

Regardless of how I dressed the package, I still had a woman's brain and heart under those men's clothes. One day she loved me, the next week I was being accused of cheating. It was literally impossible for me to cheat because she never let me out of her sight. My freedom went out the window, and we could not go out separately. Candy insisted it would open Pandora's box while all along I had no idea who that was. She turned into a control freak and I remained faithful out of fear.

When Satan comes to assassinate you, he will isolate you first.

I was secluded from my family sometimes. Mom asked some friends the name of the club I frequented on Thursday nights. My Aunt Anna and my mom came up to the gay club in West Hollywood one night to get me. Candy was on the dance floor somewhere when they found me. I left with them and curled up on Aunt Anna's couch with some hot tea. We had a cozy slumber party at Aunt Anna's house that night. My mom kidnapped her own grown daughter. I went back the next day or so. The restful sleep I had away from the tension Candy exuded was priceless. My mom was praying against that relationship. I can truly say I appreciate the fact that Mom never turned her back on me.

Every time I seemed to be on the verge of breaking up with Candy, she planned an adventure to keep me entertained. We went to Gay Pride in New York, Atlanta, several concerts, and frequented Las Vegas to gamble. It almost seemed like she could sense I was getting fed up. Not to mention, she was buying clothes, shoes, cocaine, and marijuana every Friday. She made $50 an hour as a supervisor. She even tagged me along to work with her. I began selling drugs out of the company vehicle, directing customers to meet me in various locations throughout the city.

My own "greed" for material things kept me hanging on to this rocky road of artificial love. 1 Timothy 6:9 (AMP) describes how, *those who desire to be rich fall into temptation, into a snare, into many senseless and harmful desires that plunge people into ruin and destruction.* Her insecurities got worse with time. She had the ability to stay up for days. After twenty-four hours, I would go to sleep, but her addiction had progressed to crystal meth. She became delirious and began fighting me more often.

Now, I was living in terror bottling up my emotions to avoid any confrontations. I no longer felt like the man in the relationship. I felt like a helpless, battered wife, brainwashed to stay for the sake of her sanity. She acted like she could not live without me. She would have melt downs telling me how much I impacted her life for the better. She ran one big guilt trip on me, which made me feel trapped and obligated to stay.

Going into year three, I realized I had been bamboozled. I was trying to figure out how I could get away from this unbalanced woman. I really knew by year two, I was not happy and we were not a match. She lured me in from the early stages with that traumatic rape story, so I did not want to hurt her. Her family really liked me and her cousin Pita and I had grown close. I also felt sorry for Candy because she never seemed to heal from the death of her mother. We slept on her deceased mother's mattress because she claimed it still had her scent.

The entire relationship had become a downward spiral. Every few months, Candy was either loud talking me at the club or chasing me out of the house. One occasion, I jumped a gate and hid under a car as she drove around looking for me. My mom picked me up from a burger stand as I was covered in oil after rolling under a truck. Mom never understood why I went back maybe three days later. It was a stronghold that lured me back into toxicity.

Fear has tormenting mind control.

Crazy ole Candy Snow always said that when I cut my hair back off when we started dating, that she kept some of it and made a voodoo doll. I was not sure if this was another wild tale, because it seemed impossible to disconnect from her. Another time, we fought in a store parking lot. I slammed her hand in the door and broke her fingers. My mom and Aunt Anna picked me up again around 3:00 a.m. that time. She was so bold, a day later she was outside honking and yelling, "Come home!" I went right back with her like a fool, but she had my mind warped thinking she would really kill me. I hoped eventually she would get tired of me, and just let me go free with no drama. I would have rather stayed single and independent than all this bondage. She practically had turned me into a maid and a sex slave.

Ironically, I became friends with Candy's ex-girlfriend's half-sister Cannon. Cannon was from a Crip gang called 83rd Street gangsters. She reminded me of a younger version of my other buddy Rocky that was a Blood. Cannon knew how controlling Candy Snow was from observing her relationship with her sister Hennessy before she relapsed to crack. Cannon was in a similar situation with an older lady except, her girlfriend was an active, notorious gang member. We would get high on marijuana since Cannon did not use cocaine. She was never raised with her half-sister Hennessy, but they had the same father. We always talked about how we were going to celebrate when we got away from these cougars. I went with Cannon to get her first men's haircut and to buy her first strap-on from the novelty shop.

Cannon and I would go half on a bottle of Remy Martin Cognac, our favorite drink at the time. All we did was laugh and clown off the marijuana and alcohol as an outlet for our stressful relationships. Cannon was not being bullied by her girl, she just felt a little stuck because the lady was splurging on her too. Cannon was known as a fighter and hustler in the streets. Her brothers, nieces, and cousins were all from the 83rd Street Crips. Cannon was the only person Candy allowed to visit our home, and I presume it was because of their history as former in-laws. Everyone who initially thought Candy was so cool despised her due to her mistreatment of me.

One weekend, my play brother Popper had a barbecue at his house two hours outside of Los Angeles in the desert. I rode out there with some gay boys from the House of Mizrahi, which I belonged. I let Candy know where I was headed while she was at work, and she seemed to be fine with it. She disliked Popper claiming he called her a name under his breath years ago. Candy seemed to routinely have issues with anyone close to me. Her isolation tactics were becoming apparent, she was an extremely jealous partner.

The barbecue gathering was such a breath of fresh air to be able to interact without Candy. I was having the most wonderful evening. She called a few times and tried to talk my ear off. Everything seemed fine and she never said I was expected back at a certain time. I was not the driver so that was out of my control. As the night progressed, she called me from a club named Annex sounding all vibrant. After several drinks and plenty of food, most people who attended the BBQ spent the night to avoid driving the distance back home drunk. Candy threatened that I had better find my way back even if I had to catch a Metro link train. For once, I ignored her demand and decided to deal with the consequences.

She lied and told me that she packed my clothes and left them in front of my apartment where my mom resided. Of course, I panicked and was concerned that someone would steal all my belongings. I had to call and ask my mom to look beside her car, where Candy claimed there were trash bags filled with my items. My mom was kind enough to get out of her bed to get my stuff, but nothing was there. All Mom saw was one red corduroy house shoe. This woman was playing a big game to disrupt my fun. She staged it to look like my clothes were stolen and my red house shoe was all that was left behind.

I was so mad that I had to involve my mom in that foolishness once again. Candy was being childish and pulling false alarms. Her actions were enough to drive anyone to the insane asylum. I returned home the next day while she was already at work. As I entered our room, I smelled a strong aroma of bleach. All my stuff was hanging in the closet – destroyed. The carpet had spots all over it. What a high, sketchy character to ruin my clothes over something so minor. She had to hit me where it hurt, my wardrobe was my pride and joy.

I cried like a baby when I saw my stuff ruined like that. Some outfits still had the tags on them. I was thinking, 'Wow, really Candy, is this how you get down?' Even a person with common sense would have thrown it all into the bathtub to keep the bleach from dripping on the carpet. She doused that closet with bleach like gasoline to a forest fire. My feelings were so crushed I was unable to talk when I called her. She had the audacity to say, "Stop crying. I will replace them all tomorrow." She had such a nonchalant attitude, that lady was cold as a morgue.

I did not want to walk away empty-handed so I was going to stick around to get my clothes replaced. *"For where your treasure is, there your heart will be also"* (Matthew 6:21 KJV). What a mental hold she had on me. I should have used that situation as my ultimate excuse to flee from her. Using drugs and alcohol myself, I can admit my judgment was not great at all.

"Wine is a mocker, strong drink is raging: and whosoever is deceived thereby is not wise." Proverbs 20:1 (KJV)

The more years I stayed in the relationship, the fewer friends I had. She had practically run them all away. She baited them in acting nice in the beginning. Then, like a cobra snake turned on all of them. Candy loved to make it seem like my friends were seducing her behind my back. She had a gripe with every friend to make it troublesome for me to be around them. She made me feel guilty like I was taking sides. I began having to sneak around to maintain long term bonds with people, explaining that she was insecure and to pay her no attention. If she could have come between my mom and I she would have. She disliked the fact that my mom loved me regardless, and her mom was deceased for over twenty years. To upset me, she would ask when my mom was getting out of my apartment, so we could have a place to retreat sometimes away from her dad and daughter.

There is nothing more draining than emotional bondage.

Every time she talked about my mom, she would get nose bleeds like running water with strawberry sized clots. She had fender bender wreck, and on a few occasions, she was written up on her job. I kept telling my mom Candy must be crazy not to notice her demise every time she says insulting things about her. I witnessed the Bible verse come into fruition that says, *"Touch not mine anointed, and do my prophets no harm."* Psalm 105:15 (KJV)

Candy started working on the graveyard shift. We started going to the club and taking the radio inside in case she got a call. She did the most bizarre things while she was at work. The company truck had a tracking device, so she would park near a bus stop, and we would walk to the club or bar. Sometimes, she would be so sleepy we would park in a secluded area so she could take naps. I would stand outside with a clipboard doing her job writing down the bus numbers and the time of arrival. She had trained me how to do her job too – this woman had me as her personal employee.

One night, we planned to go to the lesbian after-hours called, "Hole in the Wall." This was the infamous spot we met at, which served liquor after 2:00 a.m., and had strippers until 6:00 a.m. on 95th and Normandie. That was in the hood for real, it's a wonder we were never robbed. My friend called to tell me she would hold us a place in the line, because it was wrapped around the corner. I was anxious to party and get out of the backseat of the company truck. As soon as we pulled up, Candy suddenly became drop dead sleepy. Surprisingly, she insisted that I go in and enjoy myself. I thought that was too good to be true. I did not hesitate to jump out and join my friend in line. We walked straight to the bar kinda dancing as we waited. It was packed across the bar with only one bartender working. It was going to take a while to be served on our end.

Lo and behold, ten minutes later, I was unexpectedly smacked in the back of my head. It caused a huge scene. I could not imagine who was attacking me because I had no enemies. When I turned around to defend myself, I was in disbelief. It was Candy! After paying my entry ten minutes prior, I was leaving as fast as I came. We walked to the truck arguing as she exclaimed I left her. She could not pay her entry, but the cashier was cool enough to let her find me. I did not know that she had no money with her at work. I was so confused because I knew she had just told me to go in and enjoy myself. Surely, I was getting sick of her embarrassing escapades.

The longer I slept with the enemy, the longer I lived in hell.

After six months without drugs, we gained weight waiting on her random drug test. Candy seemed to purposely do a lot of baking to blow me up. I think she wanted to make me unappealing to others. She emphasized how much she loved the weight on me, but others teased me about it, suggesting that I slow down.

Nothing that Candy ate stayed down after a laparoscopic surgery. She began to dwindle away with no strength to display much aggression. Her condition was beneficial to me because finally, I got a break from her attacks. Ultimately, she took a medical leave claiming to have cancer, but, she was malnourished.

Candy began telling me I needed to get a job and stop hustling. She was trying to make me pick up the slack for her bills. She lived above her budget. She was addicted to catalog shopping. On her payday, she got a bunch of money orders for ten dollars and mailed them to pay on every debt.

Candy made up a resume with false work history using her phone number as my last employer. She filled out several applications online. I thought nobody would ever respond, but unfortunately, someone did. I went to that interview with no enthusiasm and did not expect a good outcome. Nevertheless, I was offered the job on the spot. I believe they only hired me not to seem discriminatory against the LGBT laws. I was a service attendant writing down information about customers who brought their cars in for repairs, inspections or new tires.

From day one, they treated me unfairly on the job and spelled my name as Nicholas on my uniform shirt. It was a predominantly Hispanic work environment, so I felt they were being sarcastic when they spelled my name as that of a male. It was the company's policy not to communicate in Spanish on the job. Yet, they all talked in Spanish in front of me. I was never trained properly, so my work performance was inadequate. I just wanted a paycheck at the end of the day. Candy kept encouraging me to ride out the wave letting the chips fall where they may.

Lost My Loved Ones
My uncle Ricky was losing the long-fought battle with colon cancer. He had been suffering for years and it was now down to the wire. He was at home in hospice care with a hospital bed in the living room. He lived about an hour and a half away in Moreno Valley, but in rush hour traffic, it took three

hours inching along. Candy drove me out there to be with my family. Nobody had ever met her besides my mom. My uncle was incoherent as he lay there sedated. I was sad to see such a vibrant business man crossing over into paradise. Candy did not even have the discretion to sit down in another room. She stood right beside me at his bedside as if she knew him. My mom got irritated and told Candy to sit down. He passed away about a week later, so I was glad I had the chance to say goodbye.

Going back to work in a stressful environment while bereaved was strenuous. I was transferred to a store almost an hour away from me. I knew that was another way to shuffle me around hoping I would quit. Candy suggested that I let them fire me eventually so I could file for unemployment benefits. She kept my entire paycheck and was depositing it into her account at the credit union. I was frustrated with the reality that I was working, but not getting a dime of it. Candy smoothed over her influence by assuring me that I had everything I needed. That did not pacify me though. I was almost thirty by now and much wiser than when we met. She tried to convince me I was getting old and could not get anyone after her. I was on the brink of shaking the dust off my feet with this draining force in my life.

Candy was so late picking me up from work one day that I could have taken the bus. She never picked up the phone when I called, but two hours later she drove into the parking lot with a smudge on her forehead. I was furious that she kept me waiting so long. Her excuse was that it was Ash Wednesday, and she was getting the pope to bless her forehead. I never heard about that ritual and since when did she become a Catholic. It looked like she took one of her cigarette butts out of the ashtray and dabbed herself with it.

Our sex life had simmered down tremendously. Living in such misery, I no longer had an attraction to her. I assume she showed up late after fulfilling her fleshly desires. Her facial expression high was always an arrogant posture with her nose in the air and her neck stiff. I cannot describe it fully, but it was noticeable to me.

A month after my uncle passed away from cancer, my grandmother took ill in Georgia. My mom immediately flew back there. The doctor informed Mom that Grandma Lera had stage 4 cancer. The tumor inside her stomach was the size of a grapefruit. It was unknown how long she would live. One night as I was riding home from work, I spoke to her on the phone. After our conversation, I broke down crying when my grandmother hung up. In the pit of my stomach, I knew she was dying sooner rather than later. In less than a week, she expired quietly at her home like my uncle did in a hospital bed. Most of my family attended her funeral except me for a few reasons. I knew my mom was going to be embarrassed if I attended as a boy. On the other hand, Candy was giving off the vibe that it would be an issue between us. Most definitely, I called in for some days off work for bereavement. I was ready to quit that job.

Rest in Paradise Grandma Lera

Surprisingly, I passed my 90-day probationary period at the job. The transfer to another store was a little better. I was able to learn enough to perform satisfactorily. The mechanics and employees drank beers after the store closed on Fridays. This was becoming a fun place to work in a sense. I had good medical and dental benefits from working there. The gimmick was to tell people they needed things that were unnecessary. I felt awful about being dishonest to customers to keep the sales ratio up. The mechanics got paid $19 an hour if they flagged a certain number of hours. If they did not meet the requirements then the mechanics were paid minimum wages. I was the mediator between the mechanic and customer. I had the responsibility of being the crooked salesman.

After my fifth month there, I received some mail from the company. When I opened it, I discovered it was the formal paperwork concerning my health plan. I continued reading the information about a life insurance policy valued at $60,000. It immediately caught my attention because I never signed up for that policy. My mom always had coverage since I could remember, so I would never have agreed to extra funds being deducted from my paycheck. The more I read the policy, the more I realized that the signature was forged and Candy was the beneficiary. The hair on the back of my neck stood up. Candy had filled out the information months prior, forgot about it, and now handed over the mail to me since my name was on it. I was petrified that she was plotting to kill me for insurance money. I never asked her anything about it, but I was certainly walking away after seven years of oppression.

I strategized my escape from this lady once and for all. I had to get a third-party witness to change the beneficiary to my mom peradventure she sniped me that week. I prayed and asked God to allow me to get the courage to leave her for good. My mom kept declaring that no weapon formed against me shall prosper. The more she spoke that to me, the braver I became. Within that month, I bought a car, packed it up with my belongings, and rolled off into the sunset. I was fired from that job. Moving back to my apartment that my mom occupied sounded like heaven. I had spent seven years in a relationship that was detrimental. In the Bible, seven is the number of completion and that relationship had finally run its course.

I left the phone she bought me on the dresser to avoid any ties of exchanging money for my portion of the bill. Her cousin Pita had been a customer of mine the entire time, and we had shared things that never got back to Candy. I called to give her my new number to keep her as a customer. I mentioned to Pita that maybe, her cousin was crazy from that traumatic gang rape and the child she let her sister raise. After all those years, the truth finally came out. That gang rape story Candy told my mother and me never happened. Pita was clueless about that incident and had pictures of the sister's baby shower over twenty years ago in an album. Pita confirmed her cousin neither had a hysterectomy nor was she a cancer survivor. She was the biological mother of the son Candy claimed she birthed because of this false rape story. Candy's lies were exposed finally.

I was relieved to finally be out of her web of deception. She constantly told that rape story to strangers. It always seemed bizarre to me, but being naïve I thought it helped her to talk about it. Candy had been making up stories from the time I met her. I never even revealed that I knew she had lied about being gang raped. I remained loyal to Pita diffusing any arguments. I thought about my mother and all the other people in random conversations she told this lie to.

Once the break up was permanent, Candy let the air out of both of my mom's right-side tires. There were no nails in the tire and once my mom put air in them, she never had issues again. I could not prove it, but she is the only person I could think of who did not care about my mom. After Candy stalked me for about a few months at the clubs, she left me alone. My friends were willing to protect me if she tried to fight me. The disturbing thing was when the lease was up at our old place across town, she moved one street from me. Ironically, she had the exact address I did. The last time I saw her, she had a boyfriend who was her son's age. Later, I ran into an old co-worker of hers who told me she had been fired.

Excursions in Perversion

2010, I finally could do whatever I wanted. My desire for women after that seven-year fiasco of fury was on pause. I was very traumatized, and emotionally fragile coming out of that relationship. I was much happier being out of that situation. Mentally, I felt as if I was released from seven years of incarceration. My motive was to make up for lost time. I was anxious to party with the liberty of no restrictions.

I reconnected with all the people I considered to be my friends down through the years. Delight my tranny friend was one of them. Some people teased me saying I would be back with Candy by the next month, while others were relieved I was no longer spellbound. My two play sisters Keisha and Natasha were eager to beat her up, but I wanted no extra confusion. I was anxious to start my single life of self-navigation.

The tranny I called my sister named London passed away. We used to watch each other's back on the transsexual ho stroll. So many people liked her and were saddened by her death. I began to lose count of all the gay people who died in the LGBT community. Her death hit closer to home because of our history as friends.

I spent every night clubbing, networking, and selling drugs in West Hollywood's LGBT community. I began to meet several people from other races with prestigious jobs. They invited me into their homes for parties because I had the drugs. Changing my pattern and surroundings was refreshing to interact outside of the urban gay community, with less tension and more income. Some of the clubs in WeHo (short for West Hollywood) hosted hip hop nights. I knew all the promoters and got in free. Over the microphone, the DJ announced, "Esko is in the building." That shout out let everyone know they could buy their drugs from me.

I rotated between three multi-racial rave parties almost every weekend. One of them was a glow stick party for gay men in the heart of West Hollywood. The other one was held at a theatre with thousands of people off Hollywood Blvd. The entry fee ranged from $40-$100 depending on the DJs they flew in from different countries. The techno music, graphics on the screen, laser lights, confetti droppings, and smoke machines were captivating. Everyone was on some type of drug hopping up and down sweating. Many of the people were other nationalities. The security had the nerve to be strict about drugs. They kicked in bathroom doors if two people were in the stall together, and intercepted transactions throwing people out. Somehow, everyone still managed to be "stoned," (high). Gays, straight, bisexual, and those who would try anything. My friends from out of town loved going there. "Party Monster" was my alias and I lived up to it – I always knew where a party was.

After being at the rave held at the theatre until 6:00 a.m., we walked one block over to another one. This after-hours was predominantly patronized by Asians. It was open from 6 a.m. to 2 p.m. Sometimes, I would wake up and go there. Day or night, I was always ready to party.

I was given some liquid "G" once, not knowing what it was. I went to the club alone that morning and took a smoke break outdoors at a table. Some Asians sent a waitress to buy us all a round of drinks. One of them pulled a small water bottle from her purse and spiked the cups; thirty minutes later, I felt very weird. I was getting warm and felt like I was walking on sand. I called one of my friends to meet me in a cab and drive me home. He lived in Mid-Wilshire, ten minutes from the location. Once I told him on the way home I voluntarily drank some "G," he told me it was a date rape drug. I noticed that people were passing out all the time. Many times, they were carried out by security. I never knew where they took them. Looking back, that could have been a sex trafficking ring for all I know. There were rows of taxi cabs parked out front.

I was deemed "Legendary" in the ballroom scene. I had earned my given position walking butch realness for over ten years state to state. The commentator had made up a chant for me when they called me out. They said, "Let's go! Let's Go! Esko, Esko that party monster Eskolada." They would repeat that a few times as I walked the runway mean mugging like a thug and walking tough. I was designated the Godfather (an overseer) of the House.

A non-profit gay foundation in Los Angeles awarded me with a plaque titled "Esko Mizrahi Realness Pioneer." The award was for recognition as the first transgender to spearhead in bringing exposure to these competitions in Los Angeles; for also being the founder of Givenchy on the west coast, and the first commentator.

I had three transsexual friends who had sex reassignment surgeries to get vaginas. Money made their world go around. They had the mentality of dope dealers, but they just expressed it in a different way by selling sex. No matter what surgeries were performed, they were just extreme gay men.

One of my sex change tranny friends named Barbie died from meningitis. I took that pretty hard because we had just partied while she was in California about two weeks before. She was visiting for a photo shoot with the most notorious porn magazine for women. Those who had sex changes did not really live straight lives. They partied in LGBTQ clubs, and continued to participate in the ballroom scene with the Houses. When they wanted to deceive a man, they attended the celebrity after parties of award shows. They enjoyed the liberty of going in public unsuspected. Some were so exaggerated in their behaviors that a blind man could see that they were transsexuals. Real women are not as flamboyant as the actions they displayed.

Down Low Men
Much of married men on the "down low" who date transsexuals like the illusion of having a woman, but are obsessed with their male genitalia. A man entangled with the spirit of lust easily falls prey to homosexual encounters. Men have stronger jawlines to perform oral sex. In my opinion,

men who have gone to jail or prison have engaged in homosexual acts. They say what happens behind those walls stays there. Once released from jail, they return home attempting to adapt to heterosexual lifestyles. They meet gay men in society to be their playmates.

The gym is the number one playing field for engagement. It's like an underground bathhouse. Many married men sneak around misleading their wives that they are working out, when in fact, they are hooking up with gay men. They utilize gay dating apps called Jack'd and Grinder to converse with anyone within a 50-mile radius. The gym is considered the safest place to meet. I know this because I used to get paid to drop gay boys off at the gym to hook up with married "down low" men in the showers or saunas.

Women should not ignore the signs when their partner attempts to anally penetrate them with their penis or finger. Another red flag is him 'always' wanting to have sex from the back. He does not want to look at the female, but instead imagine being with a man looking at butt cheeks. Down low men are homophobic to throw off any suspicions about themselves. Usually there is one male friend in particular that they spend most of their time with. They are excessively groomed. The women that "down low" men date are referred to as "beards." A lot of down low men prey on overweight or unattractive women to masquerade their proclivities. An insecure woman is so eager to have a man that it is easier to run circles around her. They like beautiful women too, so do not toss your inclinations aside.

Surprisingly, many transsexuals were "tops" preferring to give anal intercourse to other men rather than receiving. It is a 'spirit of perversion' controlling the thoughts, and actions of men and women. You would think if transsexuals looked feminine, they would be the submissive partners in the bedroom. Vice versa for lesbians who passed for men being penetrated, and having children. Logically, you would assume that a person would remain heterosexual with the identity of their God-given nature. Instead, the devil has confused the minds of many to alter their appearance, represent the LGBT culture, and promote the kingdom of darkness.

It all sounds twisted, but when you cross boundaries you are capable of engaging in all sorts of activities.

One door led to another solving my curiosities. I became lustfully driven by penetrating 'so called' straight men with my strap-on penis. Naturally, no heterosexual man would pursue a girl who looked like a boy. There were so many women with feminine characteristics. Yet, these so called straight men allowed me to penetrate them. This proved they were gay on the "down low." I never thought I was pretty enough to be in a normal heterosexual relationship. Living happily ever after with a man did not seem realistic because I was dominant. Sin opens the door to a plethora of ungodly activities.

Perversion is sexual behavior or desire that is considered abnormal.

I still went to the ghetto lesbian after-hours sometimes. The lesbian circuit was broadening its horizons. Now, they had "studs" stripping and going topless with a G string on. The feminine girls loved it, but that did not interest me. Being an attractive single bachelor myself, the women were coming out of the woodwork. I dabbled a little bit with lesbian encounters, but I was not ready to seriously date again. I did feed off the attention I received from these women being attracted to me. I just wanted to make money, look good, get high, and laugh. Making up for lost time was looking promising to me.

Cannon dumped her girlfriend before I did so she was well on her way to building an empire. She was doing big things out on the streets. She picked me up in a brand-new luxury car paid in full off the dealership lot. I invested $700 in half a bottle of Oxycontin pills with Cannon, expecting a $4500 return. Of course, that sounded like a great deal when she offered. I was slacking up on my hustle at gay clubs hanging out with her. I figured the investment would overcompensate for my partying.

I targeted people in wheelchairs who were prescribed Oxycontin medicine and were willing to sell it. I was so happy Cannon and I could hang out more often unsupervised. We were like two peas in a pod now. We went from splitting the cost of a pint at the liquor store to her buying sections at the club. I was never one to frequent straight clubs in Hollywood. I always partied in the designated gay area called West Hollywood on Santa Monica Blvd. We were now up on Sunset and Hollywood Blvd where the entertainers partied. I met women in these settings easily. I had a charming personality that caused people to be drawn to me.

In May 2010, I ran back into my old girlfriend Nancy who got saved at my church, but took me off track the first time. Nancy was dating a woman who lived two hours away during the week on the Navy base. I assume the idle time Nancy had on her hands had her sexually unfulfilled. We had some mutual friends who kept us around one another often. They all could sing well and loved karaoke bars. I liked to drink and laugh so I went with them, perhaps, twice a week.

Nancy was very straight forward. I tried respecting her boundaries knowing that she was in a relationship. Her partner was not a friend of mine, but I did not want to step on anyone's toes. When I was younger, I took risks being a womanizer and luckily escaped any altercations. Nancy let the liquor get the best of her and began to express her undying feelings for me. In the heat of the moment, I bit the bait once again. We were now creeping around on a regular basis.

Nancy had a taco party one Thursday at her apartment. She invited me and thought her girlfriend would not know. Everyone coming to the gathering were only friends of Nancy's. Without our knowledge, someone took a photo at the gathering while Nancy and I were sitting in the background at the table. They put the picture on social media not giving any thought to us, because in all actuality no one knew we were sleeping together.

The same night, we all went to karaoke and got drunk. We went back to Keisha's house to go to sleep, but she had a full house with no more blankets. We decided to go back to Nancy's apartment since she would not be expecting her girlfriend to come until Friday evening. Technically, it was Friday morning around 3:30 a.m. when we left to go to Inglewood.

Tragedy Strikes

We were up for about an hour talking, and I was attempting to get freaky with Nancy, but she suggested we wait until we woke up. She was not bold enough to invite me into her bedroom. We snuggled up on the couch with a blanket and were dozing off to sleep. Suddenly, there was an abrupt jiggling of her doorknob and a boisterous entry.

"I knew it," said her girlfriend, snatching off the blanket causing us to jump up.

"It's not what it looks like. I was too drunk to drive so she drove me here," I said.

As I quickly got dressed, the girlfriend headed toward the mantle where her Samurai swords were. Nancy tackled her stud girlfriend, restraining her in a bear hug. "Take it up with me," Nancy said. I ran out the apartment not even lacing my shoes. I tried leaping down a few steps at the end, but I fell on my right side. My arm popped out of the socket and my ankle seemed twisted. I put my arm up in the air to pop it back in socket and hobbled to the car. As soon as I started the ignition the girlfriend was outside watching me drive off.

My adrenaline was pumping as I drove fifteen minutes across town with my right foot lightly placed on the accelerator. I pulled my car into my garage space and decided not to put too much weight on my ankle. I walked on the ball of my foot. That was a big mistake because I heard a pop and my leg seemed to snap knocking me off my feet. I sat in the alley unable to get up. I called upstairs on the phone to my mom to help me. I assured her that I was ok, but I was injured elsewhere.

Mom's missionary friend I called Aunt K was visiting for a few days, so they both came down to help me into my mom's car. They drove me to the emergency room and then got a wheelchair to take me in. I had broken my ankle on both sides. The first fracture was from the fall, and the second was from putting my weight on it. I was high on cocaine so they waited a day to perform the surgery. They monitored my heart on the EKG machine.

I was in the hospital for a week. The surgery left me with permanent hardware; a plate on the left side of my ankle and pins on the right side. I had to keep my foot elevated off my heel to prevent pressure sores. The first few weeks of recovery were very uncomfortable. My right arm was not broken, but sprained, so I could not use crutches. Once I was discharged from the hospital, I had to use a walker.

I figured out after a month how to get around on my ankle. I cut my apartment window screen to throw out my gate key to customers, so they could come upstairs to buy drugs. My mom had a trip already planned and she left after my surgery. I started sliding down the steps on my behind with one tennis shoe on to run errands. I was driving with my left foot, and kicking my right leg across the passenger seat. Once I got on the crutches, I was at the clubs again. One of the chief members from the gang I was affiliated with had gotten shot, and was a paraplegic, so I borrowed his wheelchair. I was determined not to miss Long Beach Gay Pride that year.

Keisha's son Jeckle was like a nephew to me and was all grown up now. I helped her raise him since he was four years old. He had recently celebrated his twenty-first birthday. I started taking him with me to the club to watch my back since my ankle was messed up. He was a notorious gang member with a short-fused temper. I loved how he was not homophobic as long as nobody tried being fruity with him. His nickname was Jeckle from 79th Street Family Swan Bloods. Jeckle had a stud best friend name G-Main from F.S.B. too. I knew many of them from being in the neighborhood with Rocky for several years. I was so involved with them, they insisted I was from their gang. I spent the night in the dope spots with them, hung out on the block, and went to celebrations on July 9th, which was the gang's anniversary. All gangs celebrated their existence in the month that the street began, and the date was based on the number it ended with. So that's why 79th Street was every July 9th, the seventh month and ninth day.

Jeckle and I were planning to go "turn up" (party) one night at the after-hours. He liked the lesbian spot Hole in the Wall. I picked him up on the way to meet a customer and he told me to let him put his gun in the trunk. I was hesitant, but he assured me if we got pulled over he would take full responsibility. As my stud friend and her male cousin approached the car, Jeckle got in the backseat and so did the other guy. Jeckle 'banged' on him, which means he asked what gang he was from. The dude said he was from some Crip gang in Long Beach that we had never heard of.
"Never heard of them, I'm from Swan," Jeckle said.

The guy said the name of his hood again, and Jeckle punched him. They started fighting in the backseat like cats and dogs. Finally, the guy jumped out of the car and my friend did too. I just drove off without even making the transaction.

That should have been a clear indication to call it a night at 3:00 a.m. We were just getting started though. I was amped for the after-hours, and he was too. I was a little shaken up from the altercation and suggested we go back to his house to drink there instead. He convinced me that we were cool, and should not let that kill our vibe.

We were denied entry into the after-hours being told we were too intoxicated. We walked off mad as I was on my crutches. We decided to at least sit on the hood of the car to flirt with the ladies going in. Five minutes after what is called "parking lot pimpin" we encountered a crackhead asking for a lighter. Jeckle snapped at the man.
"Keep it moving. We ain't got no lighter," he said.
"This is a public sidewalk. I ain't gotta go nowhere," the crackhead said.

Jeckle punched the man, and they began to fight. I was trying to get out of harm's way off my leg to the opposite side of the car. Jeckle was beating the crackhead up, but the man kept coming back for more. Jeckle was tapping on the car. "Pop the trunk," he said. I went to open the driver's side door, but it was locked with my keys inside. That was nobody but Jesus causing me to be locked out of the car. I would have been an accessory to murder because of impulse.

We were stranded for hours before we could reach someone to help us. My crutch would not even bust the window out. We had plenty of time to sober up. Jeckle never remembered the first fight that occurred in the backseat. He told me before I picked him up he drank three bottles of cheap alcohol with Xanax pills.

Too much liquor has caused many to make regretful decisions.

A month later, I was hanging out with Jeckle. My play sister Keisha had no control over her household anymore. Around 3:00 a.m., five of us were drinking, sniffing cocaine, and smoking marijuana. Jeckle liked ecstasy pills, but he refused to do powder, which I never influenced anyone to do anyway. Many people do not know that ecstasy has cocaine and meth in it, so it's actually worse.

Around 4:30 a.m., Jeckle asked me to take his friends back to the gang neighborhood. I agreed, but since my ankle was still in a boot, I rode in the backseat. Once we got to the eastside, they noticed a suspicious car circling around. Jeckle asked a friend if this rifle was still at his house. The friend said, "Yes, let's get off on this weird car passing through the hood."

We went and picked up a shotgun the width of my backseat. I was so high it never dawned on me I would be an accessory to a crime. As we were traveling eastbound, police officers passed by us. Usually, in that high traffic gang area, the cops would pull over a car with five people in it in the wee hours. They never made a U-turn to pull us over. I was shaking in my pants praying. That was our warning from God to go home. Everyone said immediately, "Blood drop me off." Once again, being with the wrong crowd almost landed me in the crossfire and a jail cell.

Gay Pride in Atlanta was approaching and my ankle had been in an orthopedic boot for four months. I started to get depressed thinking I would never wear a normal shoe again. Cannon was loaded in cash. She told me if I got my plane ticket, the rest of the trip was her treat. She had designed a clothing line named after our crew, but a well-known rapper from Compton stole it off Twitter.

About two weeks before the trip, I got the boot off and was back in both my tennis shoes. I had to get rid of the shoes I wore while injured. The left shoe looked worn while the right shoe was in perfect shape. After shopping for our trip, we were all excited for this venture. I had been going to Atlanta pride for years with gay boys to attend the ballroom competitions.

We all stayed in a 2-bedroom suite with Jacuzzi tubs at Palomar suites on Peachtree. Cannon took her nephew and his friend. I shared a double-room with this stud named Sin who was Cannon's cousin. Cannon had the master suite to herself. We spent most of our leisure time in the living room drinking together. The guys were wild twenty-one year old thugs, so they paid for their own suite to bring ladies back to the hotel. Our whole floor smelled like marijuana once we exited the elevator. We knew that smoking obviously was not an issue. There was a famous rapper staying there and we ran into him at the valet parking.

We had V.I.P passes to avoid any waiting in line, bought sections in the clubs, and invited strippers to hang out with us. We were the center of attention with all our jewelry, new clothes, and swag (style). Atlanta had after-hours the size of warehouses. The straight strip clubs were hype too. The popular song that summer was called, "When I die bury me inside the Gucci store."

We had a blast. Cannon ran into a stripper we knew from Los Angeles. She took her back to the hotel, and they never parted ways from that day. She totally cramped our style for the duration of the trip, harassing her about flirting. I was outdone that she would jump the broom on vacation. The stripper's name was Prissy; she was a mixed breed, beautiful woman who was one of LA's premier strippers in the gay and straight clubs.

On our last night there, they decided to stay in after four days of non-stop clubbing. It was Labor Day, and I was not about to stay at the hotel while they wanted to be on a fake honeymoon. I took the rental car using GPS to navigate to the ball. I walked the ball and won my butch realness category that night. Once I connected with the gay boys, I found more cocaine and my trip needed an extension.

I ended up letting them go back to California while I stayed behind. I knew tons of people down there including family members in case of an emergency. My tranny friend Keana had a nice apartment there, so she had no problem letting me stay. She traveled a lot prostituting through the internet and wanted someone to watch her place while touring. Keana's place was flooded by a running toilet prior to my arrival and had some mildew. After 2 weeks, the smell was worrisome, plus, the location was not ideal for getting rides to the club. I played musical chairs and hopped over to my other good friend Nya's house.

I contacted Cannon to see what was going on with my investment in her business. She claimed I was responsible for a smoking charge at the hotel that caused her incidental deposit to be kept. Then she said they put an additional charge for housekeeping supposedly for cigarette butts in a glass. I found that to be unbelievable since they blew more marijuana smoke than a chimney. Cannon said my money was also used toward the trip. Are you kidding me? She initially said it was her treat and all I needed to do was buy a plane ticket. Wow! How ridiculous! I honestly felt since she hooked up with this stripper that she immediately started splurging on, she needed all the money she could keep. I was steadily observing her posing on social media like she was a realtor selling property for 50k.

ATL Gone Sour

Nya was a transsexual friend who visited California often, because her boyfriend lived there. We all had hung out several times partying and sightseeing. She used a drug called "Special K," which was horse tranquilizer. She was lots of fun. Nya randomly moved to Atlanta on the spur of the moment. Her apartment was newly built with great amenities in the building. Most of her neighbors in the complex were gay.

I was in Atlanta from Labor Day in September, until January for Martin Luther King weekend. I even had my mom ship clothes to me thinking I was moving there. I surely could make crazy decisions on my cocaine binges. Nya's apartment was full of visitors that partied for the entire weekend. She also prostituted, which was the common for tranny's and gay men to post ads on internet sites.

I was uneasy about hiding in the closet when a client came. She had a two-bedroom apartment where her living room separated both bedrooms. I decided to go wait in the computer lab until the client left. It started raining when I emptied the trash, so I did not walk to the other side of the complex. I went to sit on the stairwell monitoring the time. From overhearing her phone conversation, it would cost $250 for thirty minutes. I started to wonder what was taking so long. I tried calling her and two other guests in the apartment, but there was no answer.

Finally, I sat at the top step of the stairs, so I could hear the client leave. After an hour passed, I heard the door slam. As the client exited, he was cussing loud. I jerked back to hide as I peeped around the corner. He swiftly turned around, as if he felt my presence. The guy was husky, with a saddle bag, and wearing a fisherman's hat. He walked down the long hallway to use the stairs on the opposite end. I waited until his footsteps faded. To my advantage, he did not use the staircase adjacent to the apartment door. Once he vanished, I went back into the apartment.

There was stuff scattered all over the floor as if a tornado had swept through. Nya had no furniture yet. Nevertheless, everyone's belongings were emptied out of their suitcases. I assumed that when she told the client his time was up, he flipped the luggage over. I saw my digital camera on the carpet. Two Mac Book computers were in the center of the floor. I never imagined it was a robbery since the electronics were visible. No one was in the living room. "Hey, where y'all at?" I shouted.

Most of the company tiptoed out from the guest room in the back. They had zip ties around their wrists. I immediately ran back to the front door and locked it. Nya came out of her room crying with her wrist in the same plastic temporary cuffs. I had to get a pair of kitchen scissors to cut everyone loose.

Nya (the transsexual) said the client had the nerve to pay her and penetrate her. Then he got dressed, pulled a gun out of his bag, demanding a refund, and her money too. He got upset because she only had forty dollars cash, so he slapped her with the pistol. He was hoping she would reveal where her money was hidden. Earlier that day, I talked her into depositing the two thousand dollars she had in the bank. Apparently, with all the commotion, he heard the other guests and robbed them too.

I was not a victim, but I was terrified, so I could imagine how they felt. It made me uncomfortable to stay there. I felt paranoid that he might come back. As I organized my things, I noticed a square cloth at the bottom of my toiletry bag. It was a prayer cloth that my mom had put blessed oil on. Wow, I had no idea she put it in my luggage before I initially left Los Angeles.

My praying mother kept me covered out of harm's way.

The Bible says, *"The effectual fervent prayers of the righteous availeth much"* (James 5:16).

Everyone else called a ride because that horrible incident had pooped the party. I stayed there with Nya along with a drag queen friend of hers. The next day, Nya booked a plane ticket to New York. She decided not to invite dates into her home any longer. She said her regular clients were in Manhattan that paid her top dollar. She begged me to stay and wait for a security service to install an alarm. Nya promised she would return in less than a week, and left money for groceries. The market was in walking distance. I did feel safer with the idea of a state of the art alarm installed. I spent most of my nights in the computer lab, which also had a kitchen, television, and couches.

Two weeks had gone by and I had barely heard from Nya. She had a track record of being stuck in a trance on that "Special K" (horse tranquilizer). The lingo for being high on "Special K" was called "sent." It would sure take you to the moon and back. I have seen other users become incoherent with their eyes wide open, but unable to move. They would trick dates from Wall Street into sniffing "Special K" saying it was cocaine. This was a scheme among transsexuals to steal their clients' ROLEX watches while they were in a temporary comatose state. Nya would stay in her hotel working around the clock spending half her earnings on vials of "victory" another gay term for "Special K."

My mom had an urgent premonition that I needed to end my extended stay and come home. I was starting to get home sick after watching a historical event transpire on the news. I lived thirty feet from Crenshaw Blvd. A space shuttle was going to be rolled down this main street before retiring at a museum. Thousands of people from near and far were viewing this event live. I really wanted to go home, but getting there seemed impossible after blowing my money on a 4-month party. Fortunately, my Mom had a friend give her a buddy pass.

My last night in town, I managed to get a ride to the after-hours from this guy I met while there. I mingled with several people I knew, vibing with the music and purple neon lights. I got so drunk I took a seat at the bar and slumped over. He had to pick me up and carry me out of there. Everyone said I left the city with a bang.

My cousin Nisha agreed to take me to the airport the next morning. I fell asleep in the bathroom with my phone charging in another room. Eventually, I woke up and saw several missed calls from her. Flying on standby with the pass, I could arrive at the airport at anytime. I dreaded that my irresponsibility caused me to be stranded. I returned her call. She answered and dropped me off at Hartsfield Atlanta airport. Goodbye Georgia peaches!

The night after making it home, my uncle was murdered down in Atlanta. I never had a chance to visit him while there due to the circumstances. I was sad and grateful it was not me. My Mom had to go preach at her brother's funeral. I was unable to attend, but I poured out a little liquor in his memory. The transsexual Keana, where I stayed temporarily house-sitting in Atlanta died also. The mold in her apartment from the toilet flooding caused her breathing to be compromised. She had been on an oxygen machine for months while awaiting surgery. Once she went under the anesthesia she did not wake up during her procedure. That took me by surprise as well.

I Dodged the Bullet

Returning to California, the party escalated to a larger scale. Cannon picked up the tab at Crustacean in Beverly Hills, BOA Steakhouse on Sunset, Benihana, P.F. Chang's and many more upscale restaurants. We continued to frequent VIP sections in Hollywood's largest 'straight' nightclubs. A daytime party called 'Toxic' was the wildest event I ever experienced. We paid the security a thousand dollars to avoid the line. The section was $2,000 and they spent an additional $3,000 on bottles of alcohol. Clubs made a fortune on bottles, selling them for $600-$1,000 or more, but they were ordinarily fifty dollars at the liquor store.

There were stripper poles all over this outdoor club. White leather sectionals were in the VIP areas for those who bought bottle service. There was a stage with the DJ and performers. It was about fifteen of us in our section. Our other stud friend from the valley area ran into someone she knew who had 'mollies' aka 'moon rocks.' Cannon was strictly a marijuana smoker. The party was so off the Richter scale, we all agreed to split some mollies. That was the new ecstasy in a capsule form. Technically, it was meth in a capsule advertised another way.

Whoa! We were taken by storm on that 'molly.' We sprinkled it in our drinks feeling the effects twenty minutes later. We could not stop dancing. I was hanging from the canopy tent pole. All of us were extremely rowdy, throwing up gang signs, and feeling invincible. Cannon had smuggled in a pistol, so I was unbothered about us getting into trouble with anyone. We were not making a spectacle of ourselves because the whole party was "turnt up" (wild). Dudes were coming out of their shirt flexing muscles. Women were on the stripper poles. It lasted from at least 3:00 p.m. until 10:00 p.m. We consumed so much liquor, but it no effect on that molly.

All our costly escapades were posted on social media. Ding Dong, another stud, was one of Cannon's workers out of town running the pill operation. I overheard her saying on the phone she was missing out on all the fun. Ding Dong was overweight with rotten front teeth. She really did not like me, and had no other option but to tolerate me. I sensed a streak of jealousy from her. I think she hated that Cannon took me everywhere because I was tons of fun. I was confident, humorous, carefree, and high all the time. I would not think twice about approaching women, all they could say was "No." Cannon was living with Prissy, but I was the decoy who got the numbers from the ladies she pointed out.

It seemed as if after Ding Dong returned for a week or two, we never went out clubbing. Cannon bought me a section in the club for my birthday. Ding Dong had a temper tantrum about that. Cannon's best friend was a feminine gang banger who beat Ding Dong up in a drive thru while headed to my birthday party. They told her she could stay in the car, get a cab home, or come in to enjoy herself. Many of my friends were gay boys, and Cannon never criticized me about it. She compromised and came to clubs with me sometimes. The gay boys mistook her for a boy too, but she never entertained their flirtation one bit.

I needed a new connection for some ecstasy pills. Cannon suggested that I ask Ding Dong. When I called her, she was out of town, as usual, working for Cannon. She said a guy named Tee sold them. Ding Dong gave me his number and told me to use her as a referral. After trying mollies', I was on a hunt for them, but it was difficult to track down the capsules. I settled for the colored aspirin-looking cartoon character pills that had been on the market for years. Tee was not too far from me in Inglewood, near Manchester and Eucalyptus. I met him in a fast food parking lot. We always made the exchange with no conversation.

I was hanging out a lot with several circles of people from all walks of life. My nephew Jeckle, who kept me on some thug missions, was my sidekick. Cannon was more on a money mission, but would still fight or shoot in an instant. The gay boys were my getaway to get high and "kee kee" (laugh).

One-night stands were keeping my lustful desires satisfied. I never got back in a relationship. Pursuing love was not a priority, I just wanted options. I was chasing the dream of being a gay rapper or big-time drug distributor. I recorded a few songs talking about explicit gay subjects. My buddy in North Hollywood had a studio so it was free to make music.

The new peach flavored vodka had just surfaced in the stores. Cannon had been ordering it at clubs as our choice of alcohol. Ding Dong was home for the holiday, so we were going to meet up at her apartment to have some drinks. Initially, they were introduced while dating two sisters. Previously, things had leaked back to Cannon's ex causing her car to be scratched up. She never wanted to risk her property being vandalized again. Once Cannon moved into a house, she decided not to allow Ding Dong to know her new address. I was going to spend the night as I often did at Cannon's. Her girlfriend was going to be cooking all night while we watched movies, smoked marijuana, and laughed. That was our regular routine on any given day as Cannon's girlfriend went to bed early for nursing school.

It was the year 2010, on Thanksgiving Eve. I had my overnight bag in my trunk. Cannon called and said she was headed to Ding Dong's. I told her I was going to pick up a batch of ecstasy pills from Tee and be right over. I called Tee to make the arrangements, but I procrastinated on social media before leaving my house. When I got outside of Tee's house, I did not see his car. I called him, and he told me that he would be back in fifteen minutes. I pulled around the corner to be discreet.

Once he returned, he seemed a little anxious and unusually talkative. I was surprised he had lingered for a minute. Normally, he would pass the pills and walk away. This time, he leaned over with his arms folded, resting on my driver door staring at me. I felt a little weird that he had come so close into my personal space.

"Where are you about to go?" Tee asked.

I cheerfully replied, "Oh, I'm heading over to Ding Dong's house. Do you still talk to her?" I asked.

"Yeah, that's my cousin," Tee said.

I noticed his teeth were jagged like shark teeth and twisted. I never knew Tee and Ding Dong were related until that night. I thought nothing of it.

"Alright man, thanks, see you later," I said.

He hesitated before lifting himself off my door just staring. I drove off.

My nephew Jeckle and a customer called me a few minutes apart. My money took precedence over Jeckle wanting a ride home from the east side. Everyone wanted cocaine or pills on holidays and that big order was worth the detour. I figured that Cannon and Ding Dong would have to start drinking without me. When I dropped Jeckle off, my stud friend S was visiting Keisha, Jeckle's mom. I convinced her to follow me in her car to have a drink with Cannon.

We hopped on the freeway as I dialed Cannon to inform her we were coming. Surprisingly, she did not answer the phone. I called S following behind me to let her know the plans had changed.

"Yo S, Cannon is not picking up, let's connect again soon bro. Be safe with all these checkpoints," I said.

"Okay bro, be safe," S said.

Although I was supposed to spend the night at Cannon's house, I did not want to just show up at her door if she was not answering my call. I exited the freeway to return to Keisha's to drink my peach flavored vodka. I called Ding Dong to see if she would answer. The first time she did not pick up either. I called back, and she picked up sounding annoyed. "Party over," Ding Dong said, hanging up abruptly with an echoed background. I was thinking, wow what could have changed in one hour?

Once I got back to Keisha's house we began to sip cocktails in her room listening to music. My phone rang, as I glanced down it was Tee. I saw no reason to answer because we had made our exchange already. He called back maybe 20 minutes later and I ignored him again. I speculated he was going to say the money I handed him was not all there. I disregarded that thought since I knew I had counted it. The third time he called, I frustratingly answered. He sounded startled and intoxicated. "Oops! I called you by mistake," Tee said. I will never forget, it was 12:44 a.m. As soon as he hung up, Ding Dong also called at 12:44 a.m. I picked up and she was crying. "Esko! Cannon got shot. Meet us at the hospital," she said. I was startled to the core and concerned about the well-being of my friend.

The hospital was in Torrance, which was about 25 minutes away. There were sobriety checkpoints set up throughout the city on Thanksgiving Eve. Immediately, I called my mom to tell her what happened. She instructed me to wait, so she could drive me out there in her car. That was a relief because my nerves were uneasy, and I was also tipsy. I left my car parked at Keisha's.

We got to the hospital, and it was packed in the lobby. Cannon had a big close-knit family. Her mom was there, her son, brother, girlfriend, host of relatives, and friends in her gang. People were out in the parking lot drinking, smoking, and looking worried. Ding Dong looked strange as she paced from the lobby to the parking lot. As my mom sat quietly, people seemed to gravitate to her. They were giving her bits and pieces of the story.

I went out to the parking lot to talk to her brother in a wheelchair. He was a hustler and gang member who got paralyzed in a freak accident. He looked in a state of shock and suspicious, in my opinion. As I re-entered the hospital to check on my mom I was approached by Ding Dong.

"Hey, you got a cigarette?" Ding Dong asked.

I reached in my pocket to hand her one. She began to surmise who could have done this.

"Esko, you do not know what's going on. Cannon has a lot of women coming over to my apartment. One of them could have set her up," Ding Dong said.

"Oh wow, sounds pretty interesting," I said.

I thought that was nonsense right away. The only side chick Cannon had was my friend Sky. Ding Dong's story was a lie. Cannon loved the woman she lived with and barely had time for the one on the side. I cut her chatter short and went back into the hospital.

Cannon's mom had returned from checking on her. Her mom really liked me and was a nice lady. I went over to ask her if Cannon was going to be okay. She told me that she was shot in her eye. I told her that my mom was an evangelist and asked if she could go back there to pray before they took her into surgery. She was in total agreement. They were only letting one person in at a time. As soon as Cannon's eight-year old son came from seeing his mom, Cannon's mother announced that nobody would visit her daughter until the woman of God prayed for her.

First, we all gathered in a circle as my mom led the prayer. My mom took her blessed oil, which she carried in her purse and went to the back to pray for my friend. I went in after my mom, and Cannon was laying there with her eye covered. She was conscious and talking with a weak tone of voice. I touched her hand.

"I love you. I am glad you are okay bro," I said.

"Thank you, love you too bro," Cannon said.

I walked out of the room very sober minded. All I could think about was how I was supposed to be with her.

God showed me favor in the dark.

The next day was Thanksgiving and I returned to the hospital along with Cannon's girlfriend Prissy, her best friend, and her niece. I was still shaken by this misfortune. Cannon had successfully come out of surgery with no fluid on her brain. I got the opportunity to hear the story for the first time. Cannon was sitting up in the bed wide awake when I walked in. Her eye had to be removed in surgery.

She relayed what happened, "Last night I took a bottle of peach flavored vodka over to Ding Dong's as we had planned. After it took Esko so long to come, I was ready to go home. Ding Dong started horse playing and hid one of my tennis shoes from me. I finally got my shoe back about fifteen minutes later, I went home. After I parked in my driveway and got out of my girlfriend's Lexus, three masked people approached me with guns. I noticed one had breasts. A guy said, 'Take us inside and give us the money.' I refused and said, 'No, if you are going to kill me, do it. I have a house full of company and kids in my house for Thanksgiving.' They ordered me to get in the trunk of my car, and I refused," Cannon said.

"Wow," I said.

"What the hell," her niece said.

"Next they put me in the passenger's seat of the Lexus with a guy sharing the front seat with me. The stud got in the driver's seat never adjusting it, and the third guy sat in the back seat behind me. They put a pillowcase over my head and drove around as the dude in the back seat started asking for the money? I kept denying having any money. They threatened to rape me, burn me with cigarettes, and hold me hostage until after the holiday when the bank was open. I refused to tell them where the money they referred to was. They called people on the phone saying, 'We got her.' The robbers were not prepared for their plan to resort to interrogation. They figured I would have allowed them entry into my house, and given up my stash. They became frustrated driving around almost an hour in the car close to midnight," Cannon said.

"Man, this sounds scary," I said.

As Cannon told the story, I was thinking, 'where are the police when you need them? Nobody noticed a person in the front seat with a pillowcase and another passenger crammed beside her?'

She continued to elaborate on the incident.

"They started mentioning Ding Dong's name to me. They asked, 'Where is the money? You wanted Ding Dong to find more Oxycontin pills.' I acted clueless. Then they threatened to hurt my son and knew his name. My listening ability was keen since I could not see. The stud's voice was raspy with a distinctly manly tone. I remember that the guy who asked where the money was as they walked up had a messed-up set of teeth talking through the ski mask. The other guy used hand signals like he wanted to conceal his voice as if I knew him. As they drove around, I recall traveling a curvy, downward road with several speed bumps. They kept conversing amongst each other where they would take me. They called a few people on the phone seeking advice. I decided I would run when they got to their destination. Finally, when we got to the residence where I would be held for ransom, I snatched the pillow case off my head and took off. The stud chased me, and I fell. Then I quickly rolled under a car and pulled my head up into the engine trying to hide. The stud fired underneath and the fragments ricocheted off the pavement into my eye. The girl ran off saying, 'Let's go, I got her.' I knocked on a few doors seeking help. The last person left me on the porch and called an ambulance," Cannon said.

The whole time I listened to the details of this incident, it sounded fishy. I started thinking about my interactions with Tee. My facial expression showed I was perplexed.

"Esko, what are you thinking? Don't lie!" her niece said.

I did not want to surmise and be wrong making false accusations. All eyes were staring at me.

I told them I had a gut feeling Ding Dong and her cousin were involved. I explained that Tee asked me where I was going after I left his house that night. I noticed how jagged and twisted his teeth were too. Cannon mentioned Ding Dong hid her shoe probably to stall her. Ding Dong wanted to give Tee enough time to get over there to follow her home. I also recalled how strange it was that he called me several times that night. Ironically, Ding Dong called with the bad news seconds after Tee claimed he pocket-dialed me. When Cannon said they were driving on a winding street with speed bumps, I figured that was the street that led to Tee's alternate location next to the Inglewood Cemetery. I told them all that came to mind.

What Ding Dong said in the hospital parking lot to throw me off, crossed my mind, but I did not mention it in front of Cannon's girlfriend. Everyone agreed that Ding Dong was involved. The only way these people would mention Cannon's son and know she counted money with Ding Dong was if it was an inside job. I was not aware until that day Cannon and Ding Dong counted one hundred thousand dollars cash together. Then the very next day, some people attempted to rob her. It was all coming together fast. We had a good idea who was behind the plot. The robbers walked away with Cannon's diamond necklace, watch, and earrings, but the jackpot was never found. I know they had to be furious the robbery did not go as planned. It crossed my mind how guilty her brother looked as well, but I did not mention that.

I sure would have liked some Thanksgiving turkey. I felt as a friend I should not leave Cannon's bedside until visiting hours were over. Ding Dong showed up in the evening. Cannon's family confronted her about why the robber's mentioned her name. She stuttered terribly in her response. I kept a blank expression on my face and looked straight ahead giving no clue I was on to her betrayal. Cannon was scheduled to be released from the hospital the next day.

I was paranoid wondering if my safety would now be in jeopardy. Ding Dong knew how close Cannon and I were. I was hoping they would not assume the money was at my house. Oddly, Ding Dong started calling me to ask for a ride because the car Cannon loaned to her had been taken back. I was playing it cool making excuses. She even suggested that the two of us go to the club and scout out the silver Pontiac Cannon said the people got out of when they kidnapped her. I avoided Ding Dong by any means necessary.

Cannon was staying in her other house she bought way in San Jacinto, Ca. I told her how Ding Dong was attempting to lure me. Cannon sternly instructed me to stay clear of her. She sent her girlfriend to pick me up to visit a few days while recuperating. I went with her to her doctor's appointment to get her prosthetic eye.

The guy Tee, Ding Dong's cousin called me. I was leery about answering, but I picked up the phone acting normal with him.

"I was calling to let you know I sell powder cocaine now too," Tee said.

"Oh cool, I will be calling you soon," I said.

I hung up feeling like they were out to get me now. Tee knew I was the only one in the circle who met him. He had become so comfortable with me, I had started meeting him at his house. We also met at another spot where he hung out. The way everyone eased away from Ding Dong, they knew without it being said there was a problem. I just wanted to stay clear of it. Eventually, I blocked him and Ding Dong.

Ding Dong popped up with a car that got impounded the same day and went to jail. Then she was brutally beat by Cannon. I saw posts on social media that her brother was murdered in some projects. I have no idea what Tee's fate was. I never did business with him again. Jealousy and greed made the crew's empire come to a halt. God had protected me once again by detouring me from being with Cannon at the time she was kidnapped.

Las Vegas Chronicles

My tranny bestie Cee Cee, and I had been to Vegas for Gay Pride together a few times. LGBT pride in Las Vegas has party buses every year. We always were the life of the party. Our friend dated the man who sponsored the events. We would all ride in an exclusive party shuttle stocked with top shelf liquor. We arrived at the parties already tipsy from the party bus. One year, the annual all black party was epic when we made a grand entrance. Two gay boys who were good friends of ours accompanied us to the party. We all looked like we were headed to a magazine shoot. It looked like the everything paused when we stood at the top of the steps. Cee Cee wore a see-through cat suit to the event. That was one of the last parties I can really reflect on where we shared a memory.

Cee Cee wanted to go back to Las Vegas in November for a regular trip to celebrate our birthdays which were two weeks apart. We had planned this excursion for at least four months. Since she lived in New York, she flew to Los Angeles to put up her ad for a week. Then we partied at the after-hours in Hollywood that everyone anticipated visiting when coming to town. She rented a car so we could drive the 4-hour road trip to Vegas during the following week.

Four of us went on this birthday trip back to Las Vegas. We stopped at the marijuana dispensary. I did not put any money toward that purchase because I had no plans of smoking. It was my birthday celebration, and I wanted to be wide awake off cocaine and ecstasy pills. We gambled a little on the slot machines when we arrived. Our hotel room was nice as well. We walked the strip sipping these big tubular slushy alcohol beverages called Hurricanes. I loved the colorful lights Las Vegas Strip displayed like Time Square in New York.

One evening, we decided to go to the only gay club in the city. The gay boy took one of the tall medicine bottles of marijuana with him. I thought to myself, 'how much do they plan to smoke?' I took my cocaine and a few ecstasy pills with me – in case any of them wanted to get on my level. We had a great time and met some cool people that night.

Leaving the club, they rolled a blunt, which is marijuana in cigar paper. We were going back to our hotel to gamble. The radio was blasting as we sang along. They passed the marijuana around to each other. The car windows were rolled up so the smoke was thick inside the vehicle. We made a turn onto the Las Vegas Strip, and noticed a police car waiting for the lights to change. Immediately, we started rolling the windows down to air out the clouds of smoke.

The officer must have seen us two blocks back and intended to catch up to us. He zoomed up behind us with the siren lights on. I stashed my small bag of coke in my sports bra. The gay boy in the backseat beside me had the marijuana. I did not think that was a concern because he had a cannabis card. 'What happens in Vegas stays in Vegas,' was the slogan for the city. Prostitution is legal so the last thing I thought Las Vegas considered illegal was marijuana.

The officer approached the car inhaling very deep breaths making it obvious he smelled the aroma of marijuana.

"Have you been smoking marijuana?" he asked.

"Well, officer, we did earlier," My bestie Cee Cee said, since she was driving.

"You are not honest ma'am. I saw smoke in the car back when you crossed me at the intersection. I need everyone's ID," he said.

At that moment, I knew we were being interrogated for dishonesty. He walked back to his car to see if any of us had warrants. I became so nervous.

As he returned to the car, he was confused about our gender. He stared at Cee Cee who looked like a woman, and I was sitting behind her looking like a boy. Our licenses revealed the opposite. He asked how we all knew each other since we were from different states. We explained that we came to celebrate our birthdays in Vegas.

"Are there any drugs or weapons in the vehicle?" the officer asked.

"No officer," Cee Cee replied.

"I need everyone to step out of the car to search the vehicle," he said.

I had an open cup of alcohol that I had kicked under the seat. We were rowed across the front of the police car. It was cold standing out in the brisk night air at 4:00 a.m. I began to shuffle through my pockets quickly as the officer was occupied searching our car. I realized some loose ecstasy pills were in my front pocket. Quickly, I threw them to the ground and kicked them under the police car. He summoned me over to the curb side.

"Your buddy back there sitting with you denied ownership of this marijuana. It was only the two of you back there. So, if you do not claim it, I'm taking everybody to jail," the officer said.

I was inwardly shivering when he said jail. I knew I had that cocaine stashed on me. This weed was opening a can of worms that could have made matters worse for me. I agreed to take the blame for the marijuana and was issued a ticket. Cee Cee was cited for speeding. Finally, after an hour of freezing out in the cold, we were free to go.

God blocked it!

As we looked up, we noticed we were two buildings away from our hotel. He cited us right before we made it to our destination. After that episode, we were tired and ready to go to bed. Everyone agreed they would split the cost of the ticket I took the blame for. We had a good time the rest of our stay, but we did not move that car until we were ready to get on the freeway headed home.

Death Knocked
on My Door

Three months after I was issued that ticket in Las Vegas, I got pulled over in Los Angeles. I was told that a warrant in Vegas showed up in the system. Luckily, they did not arrest me, and advised me to take care of it. I was surprised because it had not yet exceeded the deadline for payment. Once I got home, I immediately shuffled through my mail to find that ticket. I looked in the bottom right corner and a box was marked that required a mandatory court appearance. I figured it had to be a mistake.

I called my bestie Cee Cee to ask if she had any issue paying for her speeding violation. She told me her ticket was paid for online. Nobody contributed to paying the fine for the ticket they had vowed to split four ways. I went online to the website and my ticket could not be located. I called the court and the clerk told me this ticket was a misdemeanor criminal case. I was lost for words. I thought it was mistake since it was only marijuana. She said I failed to appear in court and a warrant was out for my arrest.

Well, since that had occurred in November, and it was now February, Gay Pride was rolling back around in March. I needed to make arrangements to extend my trip to go to court. My buddy Cannon ironically had moved to Las Vegas with some woman I never met. I was looking forward to seeing my good friend because we usually hung out every day until she up and moved.

This particular year was one of the largest turn outs for Las Vegas pride. The sponsor of the event flew in people from everywhere. All the friends I accumulated in the ballroom scene were present. The cash prizes for the ball had increased. It was like a gay reunion. I knew people would love these ecstasy capsules for pride weekend. A rapper had a popular song out at the time where he said, "Popped a molly, I'm sweating wooooo!" Everyone loved to sing along in the club as they began to 'roll' (the drug kicking in).

I was thriving with excitement at this three-day event. A well-known artist was going to be performing on the weekend itinerary too. All the people who did drugs and those I partied with were in town. This was about to be a non-stop drug fest. I was splitting mollies with friends every 4 hours. I did not eat, sleep or drink any water the entire time. All I consumed was alcohol, cocaine, and mollies. If I felt sleepy, I popped another molly. I had a few sniffs of Special K, (horse tranquilizer) in settings where it was circulating. I was staying in the hotel that hosted the event. I felt I would miss something if I went to sleep. There were pool parties during the day and clubs all throughout various hotel casinos at night. I gambled in the early morning hours at slot machines, dice, and roulette tables. The waitresses walked the casino floor passing out cocktails to gamblers. By the close of my trip, I had lost $3,000 dollars mostly at the dice table.

Now that I had enjoyed my weekend to the fullest, it was time to check out of my hotel. It was Monday afternoon, and Cannon had invited me to stay with her. I was going to resolve my issue with the court for that possession charge. This gay boy from LA who was a good friend of mine lived in Las Vegas. We had hung out all weekend, so he was going to drop me off to where Cannon was staying.

I called Cannon to get her address. She said her girl was about to drop her off to the barber shop on her way to work. She told me to meet her there, and she could hop in with us so he could drop us both off to her house. My friend and I stopped at Hooters to order some chicken. As we waited for our order, I felt a little weird. I assumed my body was ready for sleep mode. I was anticipating catching up on my rest at Cannon's place.

By the time we drove to the other side of town to pick up Cannon, she was ready. I let her get in the front seat because I wanted to stretch out in the back for a nap during our commute. I was restless and irritated by the dry heat as we inched in traffic. The A/C did not work, and I was beginning to feel sick.

I was nauseous and jittery. I told them I think I needed to throw up. They said I probably was exhausted and overwhelmed by the heat. I tried lying back down. However, I sat back up because my hand felt numb. I became alarmed and emphasized to them that I was not well.

"You always go hard in the paint," (overdo it) Cannon said, laughing.

"I never felt like this man. I feel really weird bro," I said.

"Man, you just need a nap foolie, we are almost at my house," Cannon said.

A minute later, I felt a tingling sensation in my fingertips on both hands. I heard a buzzing sound in my ears like bumble bees. I panicked, insisting that I needed medical attention. Cannon called her girlfriend Prissy back in California because she was in a nursing course. She advised that I go drink some milk to cancel the effects of the drugs.

"Call 911!" I screamed, as we pulled up to the apartment complex.

"Oh no bro, the ambulance cannot come here. That's too much attention to this house," Cannon said.

My hand involuntarily closed into a claw, and my shoulder thrust upward as both locked into that position. I quickly called my play brother Popper who was a real certified nurse.

"I don't care if they drop you at the corner, call 911," Popper said.

We noticed a hospital in view driving down the road after pulling off from Cannon's apartment. We pulled up to the emergency room. I was so weak I could not stand on my own. They rushed in to get a wheelchair. Cannon rolled me to the desk and notified the clerk of my symptoms. The hospital clerk nonchalantly handed us a clipboard.

"The wait is about two hours," she said.

I laid the upward half of my body across the counter.

"Help me, please! I cannot breathe," I said, desperately.

She was not budging or attentive to my immediate need for medical attention.

Cannon got upset and wheeled me back to the car. I dialed Popper back to tell him the outcome. He told me to go down the street and dial 911 for an ambulance to assist me. There was a fast food restaurant directly across the street. They helped me into the dining area where I laid my head on a table sitting there in fear. We dialed 911. The EMT came right away within five minutes from across the street. I was honest by telling them I was abusing drugs all weekend and drinking enormous amounts of alcohol. Cannon told me to call her and hitched a ride with my friend back to her house. They put me on a stretcher and checked my vital signs as I was transported across the street. They took me on the gurney past the clerk who had just ignored my emergency.

I got to the back, but the nursing staff did not show any interest in attending to my medical needs. Instead, they were so intrigued that I was a woman they rounded up other staff to come and look at me.

"Wow, that's a girl!" they said, peeping in the curtain.

"Nothing is wrong with her. She just walked into the front. I guess she called an ambulance to cut the line," the front desk clerk said.

She had nerve to come back there with a bold face lie. I was wheeled in, and totally discombobulated with my hand locked in a claw.

Finally, the last person looked in as they pulled the curtain exiting in laughter. My chest felt like a pile of bricks had been placed on it. My breathing was compromised and I felt like my airway was closing by the second. I started praying for repentance and called my mom. I was hysterically crying as I told her I was dying. I literally felt my spirit leaving my body. The nurses were going to let me die and consider it a drug overdose. I did not even know the name of the hospital.

I mustered up the strength to get out of that hospital bed. I went and lay in the walkway begging for help. An angry nurse forcefully yanked me up by my arm and shoved me back on the bed. I began speaking in tongues as my mom went into a fervent prayer. I had an instant idea to dial 911 again. I knew those calls were recorded so, at least, my mom would have a lawsuit.

"Help please! I am from Los Angeles here alone and scared of dying in the hospital. I was transported by an ambulance. The medical staff has failed to help and making fun of my sexual orientation," I said, gasping.

"What is the name of the hospital?" the dispatcher asked.

I was unaware so I got up again.

"My mom is on the phone and needs the name of this hospital," I said.

Someone yelled it out from a desk back there. Within two minutes, there were people pulling back the curtain in a hurry. The 911 operator had called the nursing station. Now they were acting concerned. This older man with a foreign accent came in. He grabbed my hand as he stood over me.

"Ma'am, do not worry. I am going to help you," the male nurse said.

He walked off returning with an I.V. I called him my guardian angel.

The Lord just kept showing me mercy.

I blacked out and woke up five hours later, wondering what I was doing in a hospital bed. I was greeted by that same nice male nurse. He told me I was dehydrated and would be discharged shortly. I was glad to be alive, that incident scared me terribly. My organs would have shut down if those I.V.'s were not administered. I called my friend who was still at Cannon's house a mile away, and he picked me up. God was constantly so merciful to me, and my mom was such a trooper. Anytime I called her, she was instant in prayer and support. She would have driven out there if it was close enough to get to me right away.

The next day, I felt like my regular self. I had a good night's rest. I figured it would be wise to take it easy. I had no plans to use drugs or alcohol. I wanted to drink plenty of water and eat for some vitality. Cannon explained to me why the ambulance could not come to her apartment. I had no idea she had fled to Las Vegas as a fugitive. She never said what she was running from. At least, I had clarity why she left me at the hospital alone.

"Esko, you know you are a good friend bro. I was nervous wheeling you into that hospital hoping I was not asked for ID," Cannon said.

"I appreciate you for considering my well-being and believing I seriously needed help," I said.

In Las Vegas, they issued driver's licenses the same day. Since I was aware of Cannon's situation, she asked a favor of me.

"Can you call your mom and ask her to Fed Ex your birth certificate, so I can get a license in your name to prevent being arrested if I'm stopped," Cannon said.

"Okay, I sure will bro, long as I don't start getting a bunch of tickets in my name," I said.

I called my mom and asked her to send my birth certificate. We wired the money to my mom to cover the expenses for her gas and overnight shipping. The mail arrived the following day. We went straight to the Department of Motor Vehicles. Cannon was denied a driver's license in my name. The reason being, the birth certificate was not the original document. They did not accept copies. After thinking about it overnight, I was inwardly leery about doing that favor anyway. I was relieved that my name would not be used relating to my fugitive friend. That could possibly have gotten me into some trouble later after she was in custody.

I went to court and explained to the judge I was not aware a court appearance was mandatory. I attempted to get that situation resolved. A $200 fine was issued. Somehow, after returning to Los Angeles, I lost the paperwork. I never paid the ticket. All that was in vain because it reverted into a warrant later.

After my brush with death, I refrained from drugs and alcohol for a week or so. I gradually eased my way back into the routine. I returned to drinking and snorting cocaine on a daily basis. I returned from Vegas completely broke, so I certainly had to get my hustle on non-stop. I was not stressed because my rent was already paid for the year.

When you have addictions, you never consider the harm you are self-inflicting.

My play brother Popper said that I was too nice letting my mom stay at my apartment for years after her divorce. I was gone a lot so it really did not become a conflict of interest until I returned. It was a burden going to my car to smoke cigarettes. I would have friends over, but not anyone I was sleeping with. Going to hotels was becoming an extra expense. He was playing both sides, telling my mom he would talk to me if I ever made her feel uncomfortable. My heart had hardened like Pharaoh against the Israelites in the Bible. I nicely asked my mom to please find a place, so our lifestyles would not clash.

My mom moved out of state on a missionary journey. I was happy to get my apartment back to myself. All my gay friends were so sad that she left. Everyone called her mother and was drawn to the love of God in her. My mom had prayed for several friends of mine. They would share their backgrounds with her. I never heard some of the stories until they opened up to my mom at my house. Every gay male friend that I had was sexually abused and half were abused by a family member. I truly believe that when an individual is sexually violated, it opens the door to homosexuality. Perhaps, because the predator was the same sex and the victims confused the sexual stimulation as their preference. On the contrary, others are taken advantage of by the opposite sex so it draws them to members of the same sex.

Rejection is certainly the root of homosexuality.

One 4th of July weekend for Gay Pride in Los Angeles, about five of my House members came down from the Bay Area. They booked hotel rooms where the event was hosted for the after party. I stayed with them for the weekend drinking like a sailor. We partied to the extreme every time we connected. Once the weekend was over, we went to eat at an outdoor mall called 'The Grove.' It was five gay boys and me. The place was very crowded as we shuffled through people. As we were walking down the pathway between the rows of stores and restaurants, we were approached by an older lady. It literally seemed like she appeared in our face out of nowhere stopping us from going any further.

"Jesus told me to tell y'all, He is coming back!" she said, adamant.

She walked right off after she uttered one sentence. The gay boys claimed that she targeted us because of our sexuality. I did not engage in the criticism. I knew it was God speaking to me.

Soon, as we got into the restaurant to be seated, I felt strange. My palms were sweating, and I felt warm. I became alarmed because I did not want to encounter a similar episode to when I almost died three months earlier in Vegas. My fingertips became sweaty also. I told my friends that I needed to go to the hospital. They were going to be driving back six hours to Oakland after dinner. Our evening was now abruptly interrupted. I had someone drive me to a dear friend's apartment five minutes away in Hollywood. I called 911 to get an ambulance to meet me at my friend's address. I did not want to stay parked at the mall and have no ride afterward. At least, my friend could come pick me up in my car when the hospital checked me out.

They transported me to Cedar Sinai hospital. I was told that I had alcohol poisoning, with more liquor in my system than fluid. The devil was trying to kill me with drugs and alcohol. My nickname was the "Party Monster," and I lived up to that title. I began to see that I needed to slow down. I had an addictive personality that was excessive. It was time to get a hold of this problem.

Lamentations 3:22-23 (NLT) says, *"The faithful love of the Lord never ends! His mercies never cease."*

God just kept giving me chances in spite of my shortcomings.

Mom's Gay Ministry

I was surrounded by bad influences who were 'so called friends.' Three of my gay male friends and I were hanging out until the break of dawn after the nightclub. We were at Keisha's house getting high and drinking. One friend had some personal challenges that he began to vent about. The topic of the conversation shifted to God. I experienced this amongst people often, and it made me feel convicted. I did not want to talk about the Lord while intoxicated, but I noticed this happening regularly. I would tell people things that were going to happen in the future. I told my friends how I was raised in the church and filled with the Holy Spirit, but somehow got entangled with my own fleshly desires. My friends were in distress reiterating their need for prayer. My mom happened to be back in town visiting for a high school classmate's funeral. At 6:00 a.m., I called to notify her that my friends and I were coming to receive prayer.

When we arrived, my mom had a bottle of blessed oil in her hand. She did not waste any time. Mother greased her hands in that oil and placed a dab on our foreheads. She laid the palm of her right hand on our foreheads praying. We were all knocked out one by one. I was shocked everyone was laid out on the carpet speaking in tongues. My play nephew Whiz was crying and pleading with the Lord. My mom got on the floor with him, and he got filled with the Holy Ghost speaking with other tongues.

A few days later, Whiz and I went with my mom so that he could get baptized in the name of Jesus. The church we took him to that day was in Long Beach, Ca. The pastor knew me as a little girl. After church was over, we stood there rejoicing about the baptism ceremony. The pastor walked up to greet my mom.

"How is your daughter doing?" Pastor Miley asked.

"Here she is," Mom said, pointing at me.

His eyes got big, and he was lost for words.
"Hi Pastor Miley," I said.

Inwardly, I was a little embarrassed. I felt ashamed of my appearance, which I usually wore as a badge of honor in the LGBT community. God was impressing upon me that my lifestyle was not right, but he was able to fix it if I desired. I was not ready at that moment. I can honestly admit He got my attention.

This was not the first time my mom had taken my gay friends to church to get baptized and filled with the Holy Spirit. My other friend Rayna had recently got saved too. I never interfered in what God was doing with my friends. They never continued going to church to get delivered from homosexuality. God knows how to keep dealing with them because He made no mistake by saving their souls. Mom was just a vessel God used to extend His love to humanity.

Cannon moved back to Los Angeles with me temporarily. I was glad to have my good friend back in town. We would drink and smoke marijuana nightly. Her presence at my house slowed me down on using cocaine because she did not indulge. She was given a key to come and go as she pleased. She was inviting her lady acquaintances, family members, and son over sometimes. I did not mind at first, but she slowly took over my house. She had a lot of expensive jewelry and designer belts, so I refrained from my regular party atmosphere. Now that she was occupying my living room and front closet, I did not want to risk her valuables disappearing.

My friends either were coming over before the club to drink or afterward to do cocaine. I had disconnected my cable months prior because it was a waste of money. We usually listened to music, talked, and danced. Gay boys loved to practice 'vogueing' in my spacious living room. Cannon complained about there not being any cable. I figured if she felt it was a necessity she could pay for it. I explained to her that I did not watch television.

I considered her a friend, so I did not ask her for any rent. You would think having a larger economic bracket of drug sales, she would have volunteered. I understand she had been generous during our friendship paying for VIP tables in clubs, but that was for everyone in the crew. I did not feel I should be indebted to her. Technically, I never got any money on the $700 investment I made in her pills anticipating a kickback of $4,500. Nevertheless, I cherished our friendship more than holding a grudge for money. God did not intend for me to have shiploads of money living a sinful lifestyle.

For what will it profit a man if he gains the whole world, and loses his own soul. **Mark 8:36 (NKJV)**

One day, she volunteered to give me some money for staying at my house. I was appreciative that she finally was going to show the initiative to be fair. She ended up only giving me $100. Then suggested that I pay the cable bill. She would get $50,000 or more at a time. I surely would not take the money she said was a token of appreciation to pay the cable.

I rode to San Diego for the day on a business lunch date, and Cannon called.
"Aye, the cable is not on," she said.
Her tone was aggressive like she was annoyed.
"Well, you said you were giving me some money for being at my house. I was not aware there were stipulations on how I spent it," I rebutted.
"I want my money back, and I will be out of your house when I make other arrangements," Cannon said, bossily. That was an insult, she had taken her pettiness too far.
"I will be back to return your money, and you can leave immediately," I said.
Our friendship ended that day. I never saw Cannon since that night. The direction she was headed, it probably was God disconnecting the friendship.

Jeckle started taking Xanax pills combined with alcohol all the time. He displayed very erratic behavior. He lived on a busy street, which was known for prostitution in Los Angeles. Jeckle and his friends started hanging out in front of his apartment playing a morbid game called 'knock out.' It was an immature prank where people tried to see if they could knock a person out in one punch by hitting them off guard. I never stood outside with them for that game. I told him it was not cool to randomly assault innocent people.

He was always on the east side in the gang neighborhood. I was too busy chasing money to be over there daily, so we were not hanging out as often. I would visit Jeckle and his mom Keisha, but I did not take him out with me anymore. I loved this kid from the time I met him at four years old, and would have never imagined him becoming such a violent young man. He was a nice kid who wore glasses coming up. He got saved around nine-years old, afraid that he was going to hell. The same thing could be said about me going from church girl to party boy though.

Jeckle was keeping a low profile because he had committed a crime. The story he told me was that around 1:00 a.m., he was hanging out on the east side at the motorcycle club. He mixed Xanax known as 'handlebars,' with his alcohol. He walked around the corner on a side street along the club with some other gang members to smoke. Jeckle said they noticed a Mercedes Benz parked with a guy just sitting in it. They began to get suspicious among themselves wondering what the guy was up to. Jeckle approached the vehicle to ask the man if he was waiting on someone. They conversed five to ten minutes casually, and he went back to report to his friends that the guy was cool.

"Let's go back down there and rob him," the senior gang member said.

Jeckle went into the bushes to grab his pistol. The two of them walked back to the guy's car. Jeckle swung open the man's driver door, pulled the gun out and told him to get out of the car. The other unarmed senior gang member went and sat in the passenger seat of the car. The man was startled, because they had just carried on a decent conversation. He refused to get out of his car.

Jeckle began to pistol-whip him (beat him with the gun). The man still would not budge. Jeckle took the man's jewelry and wallet. The victim panicked, shifting his car in reverse knocking Jeckle down with the open door. Jeckle ended up getting a gash on his head from the corner of the door as he was knocked to the ground.

The man drove off with the other senior unarmed gang member in the car. The gang member was terrified as the man drove with excessive speed, running red lights in hopes of being pulled over. The gang member pleaded with the man to stop the car. Ultimately, the police did pull the man over for speeding. The accomplice was arrested immediately. Jeckle was rushed to the hospital to get stitches. A month later he was captured with the man's wallet and the gun.

The man was a well-known C.O.G.I.C. preacher, and he did not press charges. The district attorney prosecuted them based on the evidence found. They were both sentenced to eighteen years in prison. I was so disappointed that one wrong decision ruined his future, but I was not surprised based on the choices he was making in life. He had just had an adorable newborn baby too. Eighteen years was a harsh sentence for a first-time offender. I believe the Lord saved Jeckle's life, because he was so involved in gangs, he would have ended up dead in the streets. I took his absence hard, but it caused me to be more cautious about the company I entertained.

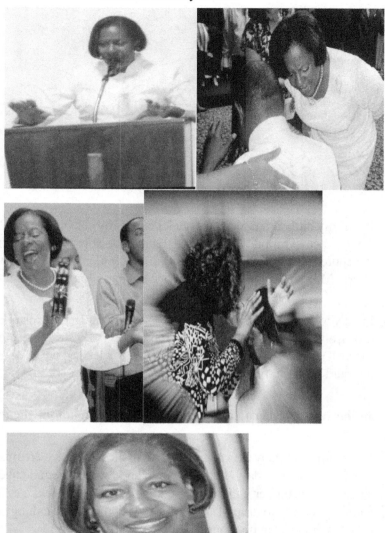

Mom in Action

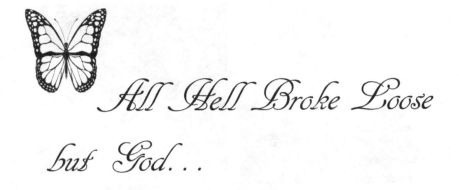

All Hell Broke Loose but God...

It was my birthday month. As usual, I began my celebrations on November 1st. My actual birthday was on the 22nd. I had several parties at nightclubs the entire month. Being high and sloppy off liquor was nothing new for the "Party Monster." I had been living one big party for twenty years.

I really took it to the extreme after that seven-year lesbian relationship. Sex, drugs, and rock n' roll was the title of my life. YOLO was my motto, which meant "You Only Live Once." You would think since we have one life that it would be in our best interest to be productive.

In this millennial era, many live for the present, not for the future.

I had some company over for drinks one night. My keys were missing when I woke up the next day. I searched high and low for them. I called Delight, since I entrusted her with the spare keys to my house and car. She kindly came right away to drop off my extra keys to me. I tried calling some of the people who were at my house, but there was no answer.

My play brother Popper changed my locks for me. Now, I had no anxiety about my original missing set. Popper brought it to my attention that I should not put the empty packaging of the case in the garbage with the sticker on it. He peeled it off because he said anyone could go buy this lock based on the sticker and the keys all were the same. Only a criminal would know that.

I ended up finding my keys in my top drawer the following day. I am certain that I rambled through that drawer looking for them. My instinct told me not to return my new spare car and house keys to Delight. I gave them to my Uncle Wendell instead, in case of another emergency.

All hell broke loose. It was like a domino effect of drama. A sex tape leaked and I was so embarrassed. I faded off the gay scene to give that time to die out. I figured, maybe, after a month or so, someone else would be the hot topic. My play sister Keisha had been acting weird. The guy she was casually dating was on meth, and he turned her out on it too. I contacted her biological sister, thinking she might be able to intervene. Keisha's newly embarked crystal meth binges made her act totally different. We went from talking a few times a day to her being missing for days.

I taught Keisha the drug trade a while back, since she was a struggling single mom with 3 children. Jeckle was over eighteen, but her daughters were young and wanted to participate in cheerleading. Since she started doing meth, when I referred customers she was unreachable. Days later, she would call back with stories of being busy having sex. Meth was a highly sexual stimulant, and it was drastically changing her behavior.

Keisha got upset that I disclosed her business to her own biological sister. I was genuinely attempting to help Keisha before she had gone too far. Her delusional mindset caused her to take her anger to the extreme. She lashed out against my character and stirred up a bunch of drama. As a friend of almost twenty years, we had gossiped about many people. She retaliated by telling people things I said about them. Of course, people only tell one side of a story and paint pictures to magnify the confusion they intend to create.

Keisha conjured up enough lies intertwined with truth to convince Delight to bite the bait. We ended up falling out and luckily, I had just got my spare keys back two weeks earlier. That rowdy tranny Delight could have driven my car to an unknown location and left it there. Then Keisha told Natasha that I said she got the shakes when she did not drink any liquor. Natasha was a functioning alcoholic who worked, but she filled up a water bottle with clear tequila to sip on the job. The "he say, she say" from Keisha spewing venom was spreading rapidly.

The past year, I had been staying the night over at Natasha's house, at least, once a week. Her girlfriend was a stud and the three of us got along very well. I loved my play sister Natasha's cooking and their place was like a getaway to rest. One morning that I stayed over, I had to move my car for street sweeping. The sign said between noon and two o'clock. When I got up, my keys were not beside my shoes as usual.

"Esko your keys are in here. I was going to move your car, but there were no parks close by so you have to park around the corner bro," Natasha yelled.

A few days later, Natasha text me while I was at home. She was cussing me out telling me what Keisha had told her. Delight had jumped on the bandwagon with Keisha adding more gossip. I tried to explain because I did value Natasha's long-term friendship. I honestly was more concerned about losing her as opposed to Keisha. Natasha and I had great laughs, we enjoyed food, and went several places together. Jeckle was already in prison, so he would have been the only reason that I would repair the misunderstanding with his mom Keisha.

Since Natasha could not hold anything confidential while drinking, she told on herself. She text a photo of my house keys showing me she had made a copy of them. I knew at that moment, the morning she claimed to attempt to move my car, she had really gone to a locksmith. I believe God was working on my behalf by forcing her to reveal this. She could have crept in while I was asleep and done anything to me. Her girlfriend was a member of the 30's Crip gang and carried a pistol everywhere she went. They had begun popping ecstasy pills nightly, so I was not sure what could have triggered their actions.

I drove to the hardware store a second time to buy new locks. I had watched Popper do it the last time. It did not appear to be difficult, but it ended up being a mystery to me. I spent hours drunk trying to change my locks alone. I passed out on my couch and woke up with my door wide open the next afternoon. At that moment, I knew that God had angels watching over me. Anyone, including my crackhead neighbors, could have come in. The man who lived underneath me was a creep, who always tried to coerce me into his apartment to look at the repairs. The other two neighbors were convicts. I ended up paying the guy across the hall $5 to install my new lock.

Jeckle's stud best friend, G-Main was hanging out with me during this turmoil. She started bringing ghetto girls to my house. Since I was avoiding the club, I had fun throwing small parties at my apartment. Instead of hanging out on the east side, some preferred to come to the west side of town. She pressured me to sleep with these blind dates. Although I was definitely lowering my preference by messing with these women, I did it anyway.

I was quarreling with some House members in a national Facebook group for members only. The Overall Father of Mizrahi, Zandy, threatened that if I continued on a rant, I would be permanently kicked out of the House (gay sorority). I *"read"* Zandy, which means got him told. All the admonition I used toward him was tea (gossip) Popper told me. I voluntarily dismissed myself from the House that I had been a part of for twenty years. I always said gay men stuck together against me, even when they were wrong. I was technically a woman, and they were all taking sides with the gay boys. I had reached my breaking point and cussed out everybody. I felt that was *"tired"* (wack) the way things went down.

Romans 1:26-32 describes the characteristics of the LGBT as being backstabbers, those who refuse to understand, who break their promises, are heartless, and have no mercy.

I was so angry and bitter about all these accusations it became overwhelming. I had no regrets resigning from my position as the godfather of the House of Mizrahi. I had earned my legendary status and needed no validation at this point. I began to realize at thirty, I had no intentions of participating in those competitions anymore. Nobody knew my age because I looked like such a young boy. Everyone assumed I was no older than twenty-five, especially with my wild actions. Due to all the trauma, I did feel stuck ten years behind.

I started speaking life over my situation without being aware of it. I began saying all the time, "I'm a God-fearing, honest woman." I would say that to my mom and she thought I was crazy to say what she could not see by my appearance. She was living in another state, so we would video chat a lot. One day, she laughed so hard when I recited it, I nearly cussed her out.

"I am a God-fearing, honest woman because I am honest, and I fear God. I'm very serious when I say it, and I find nothing funny Mom," I said.

God, who quickeneth the dead, and calleth those things which be not as though they were. Romans 4:17b (KJV)

I was parking my car over at the Baldwin Crenshaw shopping mall. All the upset people who were looking to attack me had been riding by my house. All the people Keisha contacted considered her to be obnoxious prior to this. They used to despise stopping by her house because she talked nonstop as she picked boogers out her nose, rolling them around on her fingertips. Now, instantly, their common denominator was their overnight hatred for me. It seemed like the angry mob was stalking me.

I had a vivid dream. I was asleep in the dream and my bedroom door was kicked in. I was shot twice. As I lay there with the blood gushing out of my body, I literally felt the emotion of taking my last breaths. I felt my heart racing as life left my being. I felt these things in my subconscious. I woke up overwhelmed. Warning comes before destruction. I knew I had to change my life because it would only lead to being dead or in jail.

Natasha and her girlfriend started riding by my house honking. She would yell out obscenities. The store called 'The Liquor Bank' was across the street from me. Since they sold alcohol cheaper, Natasha drove across town to this store almost every day. On her return home, they would harass me. One night, her girlfriend fired shots in the air to see if I would look out my window. I was not going near my window after gunshots were heard. At that time, I was sitting at my computer talking to my mom. I got up and tiptoed toward the back of the apartment. I felt like the entire situation was being taken too far because of gossip. The way the devil was operating through them, you would think I had stolen from them.

My long-term tranny friend Savoya from 'Five-Eleven,' who was a sex change, invited me to the straight club. It was another tranny named Rachel's birthday. I knew of this person, but we never had a close relationship. Since all this mayhem was going on in the gay circuit, I agreed to go. A night out sounded like fun after walking on eggshells the past two weeks. Rachel had just been released from jail the day before. We all rode with Savoya to this premier club called 'Greystone.' The valet parking lot was full of people waiting in line. We got in right away with a group of men who were captivated by Savoya's beauty.

After walking through the door, we never saw those men again. This club was at a big beautifully decorated, with huge chandeliers, and a bright neon sign of the club's name across the stage. Rachel immediately went to find a seat secluded in a corner. Savoya and I paraded around enjoying ourselves. I think Rachel knew she was not on the level of these women, and did not want to be clocked that she was a man. Some NFL players invited us up into their section for endless drinks. We were having an amazing night. One of the men was sharing cocaine with me in the VIP. They seemed to be a fun group of dudes. We never saw Rachel until it was time to go.

"The football player invited us to eat down the street at Berri's," Savoya said.

'Berri's' was an upscale cafe with a live DJ. I loved their lobster pizza. Although I did not have an appetite, I was willing to be social.

"Whatever you want to do is fine with me," I said.

Once we exited the club, we saw a group of foreigners standing on the sidewalk.

"Hey, where you all headed after this?" A man yelled.

"We are not sure, it's my friend Rachel's birthday," Savoya said.

We walked back to see what the man wanted as he dangled this gold Ferrari key. There were about seven people in total, all nicely dressed. The three women with them were gorgeous. The guy who approached us suggested going to the after-hours on Melrose Avenue. As soon as we seemed interested, he glanced over to his friends.

"By the time we get there and park, the liquor will no longer be served. Let's meet at my house down the street in Beverly Hills. Put my number in your phone," he said.

"Okay, I'm going to text you from the car to get the address," Savoya said.

Soon as we got to the car, Savoya called the football player we met inside the club. She had a breathalyzer DUI monitor attached to her ignition. Her car would not start unless her alcohol consumption was under a certain level. They pulled up to blow in it, assuming we were meeting them at the restaurant.

My other tranny friend Sharon from out of town called. I told her we were going to some rich man's house in Beverly Hills. Sharon asked us to swing by her hotel, so that she could come. I was the designated driver at that point. I zoomed up to the Loews Hotel to circle back to Beverly Hills from Hollywood.

When the GPS announced we had arrived, we were parked on a side street where Neiman Marcus was located off Wilshire Blvd. That was a very nice upscale area, one block over from Rodeo Drive. All the high fashion designer stores that celebrities shopped at were in close proximity. I was a 'lush' eager for a cocktail, and planning to pursue one of the exotic looking foreign women with him. Savoya called to let him know we were outside. The guy who invited us walked across the parking lot to greet us. Our car was parked at a meter on a residential street.

"Pull onto Neiman's lot, you will get a ticket on the street," he said.

"That makes no sense to me. It is not business hours. No change is required in the parking meter, and it seems odd to be the only vehicle on an empty lot after store hours," I said.

"I know the security guard," he said.

The guy called someone on the phone. He described our vehicle informing him we were his guests and to keep an eye out for the car. I pulled onto the parking lot.

We walked over to the next block to his condo. There was some music playing as we entered. The place was very plain like a bachelor pad. There were no paintings on the wall, no television, and only one small futon leather sofa. The other thing I noticed, were about thirty empty liquor bottles uniformly rowed on a coffee table. I thought to myself that all they did was drink there, and I wondered why they were saving the bottles. The small dining table was filled with an assortment of liquor with sprouts on the end. That reminded me of a club bartender.

Then, I realized there were only two guys there as opposed to the party of seven we initially saw in front of the club. I made drinks for the ladies and me. I walked over to the guy who invited us and splashed his drink.

"If this is poison, you will be having some too," I said.

He snatched away his cup.

"Oh no, I have had too much to drink. I do not need anymore," he said.

I sipped my glass noticing a strange taste. I always drank peach-flavored vodka straight. This had an aftertaste, but I continued to sip down a little more anyway.

"Where are the other ladies? Why haven't they arrived yet?" I asked.

I thought to myself, 'how could we have detoured to Hollywood to pick Sharon up, and come back to Beverly Hills beating everyone else there.'

"Oh, the other people stopped to get juice to mix with the alcohol," he said.

I noticed twenty minutes later, the other man had disappeared.

"Where did that guy go?" I asked.

"He went outside to take a phone call," he replied.

The man seemed agitated that I was so inquisitive. I had been sitting on the loveseat beside the door. His male friend never passed me to exit. I became suspicious.

"Would you like to see my Ferrari out in the back?" he asked.

"Can I drive it to get a pack of cigarettes? Otherwise, that's okay," I said, sarcastically.

I was no stranger to luxury vehicles. It seemed like he wanted to lure me off.

The three trannies were taking selfies and talking amongst themselves. Sharon did not have a sex change, but she looked just as passable as Savoya. Sharon had a very animated coke bottle shape that was probably just too perfect. The birthday girl, Rachel, looked questionable with big hands. She stomped around with her big wide ashy feet as she kicked her heels off. In the light, a prickly beard was visible.

After Rachel went into the kitchen to do some cocaine with the guy, he must have noticed she was a tranny. I got up off the couch to do some cocaine too. He looked me dead in my eyes.

"These are your sisters?" he asked.

I could tell he was a little suspicious of Sharon suddenly because he noticed Rachel was not a real woman. I looked him directly in his eyes.

"No, these are my sister's friends," I said pointing at Savoya.

He was attracted to Savoya and had no clue about her.

Suddenly, out of the clear blue, I felt an urgency to leave. I began to panic and made up a lie.

"I have to go because my girl is going to be upset if I am not home," I said.

"Esko, you are overreacting on drugs. Girl sit down honey," Sharon said. She was so eager to try to get some money out of these two men.

"Hey, what is the address so that I can call a cab?" I asked.

The man started pacing the floor. My question was ignored.

"Can I speak with you in my bedroom briefly?" he asked Savoya.

She walked to the back with him.

"Listen ladies, we are all grown. I am leaving, and you all can stay. I'm not raining on your parade honey," I said.

I walked out, glanced at the apartment number, put it in my phone. As I stood in front of the condo, I took a picture of the address, and proceeded to

Wilshire Blvd. I was going to possibly flag down a cab or bus. The spirit of death drove me out of there –something was about to transpire. Immediately, I heard a clacking sound from their heels shuffling down the walkway.

The trannies were also ready to leave, as he walked them out. We proceeded to walk across the Neiman Marcus lot to Savoya's car. Our only concern was who can blow in the breathalyzer. The guy escorted us to the car volunteering his neighbor to do it. He got on the phone and called him. Then he claimed that the neighbor was coming from the store with the rest of the group. At this point, he was acting suspicious trying to stall us. We all got in the car as I sat in the driver seat locking the doors. The guy attempted to open my door. I cracked the window.

"The neighbor is sober, here he comes," the man said.

I looked across the parking lot and there was a black jeep with tinted windows. A man in all black was getting out of the passenger side jogging toward us.

"See, here comes my neighbor," the guy said.

I cracked the window and stuck the tube out for him to blow into the breathalyzer. I started up the car and skid off. The 'so called' neighbor was never at the store. He was parked in the jeep waiting for his instructions.

The guy had anticipated we would pass out on those drinks. He told us to park in the department store lot, so the car could be easily identified for disposal. The transsexuals never sipped their drinks. I was the only fool to consume any, and after about two ounces I could not bear the aftertaste. If he had never suspected Rachel was a transsexual, we probably would be victims of sex trafficking. Once she got too comfortable taking her heels off exposing those big, ashy feet it blew our cover. Not to mention, since Rachel had just been released from jail, she was not able to have her facial hair lasered. That was all God though. The man thought he had gotten some pretty black women to make him wealthier. If anything, he would have benefited from me as a biological woman and Savoya being a sex change.

Once everyone was dropped off including me, I went right to sleep. I was in such a dark, heavy slumber it scared me. In my sleep, I began hallucinating. I was imagining myself as a ballerina in a stance on one foot with the other leg thrust up behind my back with my toe pointed. I felt like my arms went into a spread-eagle position. All I kept thinking was if I did not force myself awake I was going to die in my sleep.

In my mind, I started pleading the blood of Jesus subconsciously praying, and asking God to please wake me up. Finally, I wrestled out of that black hole of hallucination. I was drugged at that Beverly Hills condo. I was emotionally unbalanced feeling like I was coming down off an ecstasy pill. I called my good friend Christian to tell him what happened and to vent about all kinds of stuff. I even cried about missing someone's funeral ten years ago. I felt so depressed and irate. He was the friend I always called to talk me to sleep after my drug binges. In this case, I was afraid to return to sleep. I felt mentally displaced.

I recall acting a little bizarre after this incident. I was very talkative rambling a lot. Whatever that substance was, it stayed in my system for a few weeks. I kept my mom on the phone for five hours one night. I began to tell her we would be rich. I was fixated on a record deal from the two songs I recorded.

I had my own plan, but God had a purpose.

My play niece named Lisa was a tranny sex change like Savoya, with a vagina also. She called me one night.

"Uncle, let's go to this party in Hollywood Hills," Lisa said.

"Alright! Where are you? You sound like you're drunk," I said.

"I'm at the 'SLS Hotel' with some Australians buying me drinks. Meet me here so we can head to the hills," Lisa said.

"Okay fine, but I'm going to drive because you sound really tipsy, so do not leave without me Lisa," I warned.

She was not much of a drinker at all.

I was sitting home bored on my computer surfing on social media. My immediate circle of friends had turned against me, and I was still embarrassed to show my face at the gay club after the sex tape leaked. I was also tired of G-Main using my apartment to entertain ghetto women and gang members. I was keeping a low profile. The party in Hollywood Hills sounded like the perfect night out. Here I go again accepting another invite. I totally procrastinated as I was fiddling around on the computer for almost an hour. Lisa sent a text message threatening to go without me. She sent the address to meet her there. I ordered her not to leave and dashed out the door immediately. I was completely sobered that night. I had no plans until she called.

I pulled up to the hotel beside the Beverly Center. Lisa was waiting in her car for me. She rode with me and typed the address into her GPS. She had some marijuana rolled up, which we smoked on the way to the party. It was after 2:00 a.m. already.

"The text invite to this party says all night," Lisa said, as we traveled on Laurel Canyon.

It was a narrow winding road and we seemed to be driving forever.

"Call to verify the address and enquire if this event is still going on," I said.

Nobody answered the phone. The GPS said we were at our destination, but the house looked empty and dark. Lisa was so drunk, she laughed hysterically.

"Niecey, we should go home," I said.

"Oh Annie, we are almost there. I had the wrong address; it was not south, but north Laurel Canyon, which is ten minutes up the hill," Lisa replied.

As we continued this excursion, she pointed at the road Mount Olympiad.

"A celebrity I dated lives there, so yes, this party is in a lucrative neighborhood, "Lisa said.

"I cannot wait to get there to meet some wealthy people," I said.

We reached our destination as we pulled into the driveway of a beautiful home.

"Go ask for permission to park in the driveway," I said.

We were not sure if this party was still taking place, so I was sending her in first to scope things out. At the house: there was a Range Rover, Mercedes Benz, Harley Davidson motorcycle, and a Geo Prism with dark tinted windows. I spotted a surveillance camera on the roof of the house. Lisa returned to the car barely able to get a sentence out from laughing so hard.

"Annie, I don't know where I could have met these people, nobody speaks English," Lisa said.

"Was there any food left?" I asked.

I had the munchies from smoking the marijuana.

"There did not appear to be much going on. Since we drove all the way up here, let's at least go in for a moment," Lisa said.

"Yeah, I guess you're right," I said.

I had a metal hammer with a black rubber handle in my door panel. I grabbed it to place inside my pants. It might have appeared to be a gun to whomever was monitoring the camera. As we walked in, nobody was visible. The house was beautiful with pillars that had statues on them. The floors were marble, and it was expensively decorated. I started taking selfies right away. I wanted some pictures in this million-dollar home.

A guy was walking through to the kitchen and Lisa introduced me as her brother. I gave him a firm handshake with my rough dry hands. He passed us again in the living room heading down the hallway. After Lisa and I finished taking pictures together, I asked her where everyone was. She pointed in the direction that the gentleman had just walked in. As we went toward the gathering I heard loud, strange opera music. I stopped in the middle of the hallway. I observed a step-down add-on room.

"I am not going down in that room," I whispered to Lisa.

A man with long stringy hair had his back turned standing in the doorway. I could hear a foreign language being spoken over the opera music. Lisa initially said that there was supposed to be marijuana, drinks, and an all-night party. I did not even smell the aroma of cigarette smoke. I grabbed her hand firmly. "Let's go now," I said. We walked out the door and drove off.

Lisa was giggly and puzzled as to how she was invited to this gathering. We drove back to her car, and I trailed her home. I decided to stay the night since it was so late. Once we got to Lisa's house, I asked for more details about that party. By now she had sobered up a little bit, so she went back into her phone to retrieve the text message. It read verbatim, "The turn up is real all night, food, drinks, weed, and fruit." The address was included. Those people were Russians, sending out messages using urban street talk. No Black person would have mentioned fruit at a party. The fruit they were offering was forbidden. Instantly, I knew then, this was a sex trafficking scam.

Lisa worked a prostitution ad on the Internet. Since she was a sex change she posted her photos to solicit on a website for 'real women.' These foreigners thought she was a biological woman. In my assumption, since prostitutes are accustomed to going on out calls, these predators figured they would bait women in this way. It makes me wonder how many eager for a party in Hollywood Hills previously showed up to this address.

I really believe that since they thought I was a man, and we did not go into that back room, we were blessed to escape the plot of the Enemy. If I had allowed Lisa to go alone, I may have never seen her again. I was convinced there were angels assigned to my life, after encountering these sex trafficking rings twice in one month.

God was surely getting my attention by showing me I was repeating a vicious cycle of danger.

I went to the Wilcox police station in Hollywood, Ca. to notify them. They did not take me seriously at all. They asked if I was held against my will. Since I was not forced into the home or held hostage, there were no grounds for an investigation. They told me that they could not consider something based upon my instinct. Well, I tried to inform them. I felt someone could have a missing daughter. I really did have a caring heart for the well-being of others.

My birthday had arrived on November 22nd, it fell on a Saturday. Savoya invited me to a party held by the guy she was dating. He had rented this huge reception hall in the industrial area of Downtown Los Angeles. Ironically, we shared the same birth date. I dressed grown and sexy for the party on my birthday. I wore a cardigan sweater with suede elbow pads, designer jeans, and some men's low-cut boots. We were allowed to bring bottles of liquor in with us. We had a blast at the private party. It was packed, the DJ played great music, and the upstairs outdoor loft was a cool place to smoke. I mingled with some friendly people.

After I got home from the party, this gay boy name Richie called me. He had some friends over and wanted to buy some cocaine. I wanted to shower, and put on something more comfortable. He lived on the eastside in a ghetto area. I was already drunk and should have declined the money altogether.

Richie was one of those obnoxious gay boys. He was dark skinned, with braces, and a medium build. He would bully people, and try to act tough when drunk, throwing up gang signs in gay clubs. Nobody was in a gang, but he thrived off intimidation, and he met his match a few times. A lot of gay boys could fight from having to defend themselves from hate crimes.

I went over there, got high, drank more alcohol, and listened to music. His boyfriend was in the other room sleeping. His other two friends were partying with us.

"Let's go to your house because I do not want my boyfriend to wake up," Richie said.

I was getting tired as the sun was rising.

"Okay, that's fine," I said, sluggishly.

I never was one to decline a party. My addictive personality caused me to have no boundaries. I never stopped drinking or getting high. Once it was all gone, that was when my party was over.

I remember going to my car, and Richie got in the passenger seat. He ran back into his house to get his phone charger while I waited. He was taking a while, so I let my seat back. Unbeknownst to me, I dozed off to sleep. I woke up hours later with my driver side door wide open. It was hot, the sun was beaming on me, and I was sweating. I was looking around confused trying to figure out where I was, and why I awoke in this heated car. Once I glanced over at Richie on his porch steps, I realized where I was. I dug into my pockets – my bags of cocaine were missing. I checked my wallet and it was empty.

I got out to go talk to Richie. Him, Mark, and some girl were drinking and sniffing lines of cocaine off a plate. It was barely noon, and they were already intoxicated.

"My cocaine and money are gone," I said.

"Esko, you bought us all food last night. We went to the 24-hour drive-thru, and you told us to finish the rest of the cocaine," Richie said, chuckling.

"That's interesting," I said, in a catty tone.

I knew for sure that I would never have done such. I did not show generosity in that aspect. There is no way possible, I would give away the product that supported my habit and my livelihood. All this ran through my mind as I looked at this guilty grin on Richie's face.

They had the nerve to pull out the green little bags I packaged the drugs in, and offered me some as if nothing happened. I was furious, thinking how this would not be the end of this story. They robbed me blind. Then insulted my intelligence with that ridiculous lie. I left an hour after I woke up in my car to play along with their nonsense. I wanted to seek revenge, but my conscience was saying to let it go, and never hang out over there anymore.

"The way of transgressors is hard." Proverbs 13:15 (KJV)

It seemed like my decision-making got worse with time. I had no idea the effect those foreign substances had on me from that condo in Beverly Hills.

I seemed to be all over the place mentally. I was assessing my life. The direction it was going in was oppressing.

My good friend who was a gay boy name David posted a statistic on social media. He wrote on Facebook, '21 days to break a habit.' He was one of the guys my mom prayed for, when Whiz got filled with the Holy Ghost in my living room. We got high on cocaine all the time. He was simply making a statement, but I decided to try it.

Of course, I was in denial of my habit. I considered my daily consumption of drugs as recreational. That Facebook post planted a seed, and I challenged myself to see if I could achieve it. I started hash tagging '21 days to break a habit, every day of my journey. I called myself experimenting with a myth so to speak. My road to sobriety and deliverance was beginning; I did not even know it yet.

After being two weeks clean, suddenly, Delight, Keisha, Popper, and Natasha were calling my mom with identical lies. They were trying to convince her that I was using meth. My mind was clearing up out of a fog on my endeavor to be sober. Popper told my mom I needed to come stay at his house. They all knew my mom for years. All the gays called her 'Mom.' They pretended to be concerned, and asked her not to mention that they called; claiming to be giving her some inside information.

I had told my play brother Popper about how I had to change my locks again. He got so upset.
"Why did you change your locks again?" he asked.
He reacted so angrily and abrupt, it seemed strange. I became suspicious at his response. I began to analyze what he said about the sticker on the package when he changed my lock. He had peeled it off informing me that all locks with that serial number had the same keys. He was plotting against me, but was playing along like he was my friend. He cussed me out about resigning from my position in the House and insulting the founder with tea (gossip) that he told me. Furthermore, Popper convinced me to get involved

in a scam, and I backed out at the last minute. Being a single gay parent raising a bunch of kids, he was looking forward to a few thousand dollars.

After Popper's blow up, I knew then he had been holding in some frustrations. He was a gay man and had sided with his own kind. Since I was sober, I was more alert and keenly aware. I felt in my gut that he had teamed up with the others planning my demise. Popper was a gang member from Van Ness Bloods with a reputation for violence in the street. Also, in the gay circuit; the men were intimidated by his size, track record of shooting at the balls, flipping over tables, and acting crazy.

I called my mom to fill her in on all this drama that seemed to be escalating. I thought it would be wise, peradventure something happened to me. During that conversation, my mom told me they had all contacted her. She said they insisted I was displaying bizarre behavior on crystal meth. Immediately, I realized this was a plot against me. They wanted to make it seem like I got on meth and if someone assassinated me, my mother would have no idea who it was.

I began to tell Mom everything that happened, and she was shocked. They had left out all the details. When my mom said Popper emphasized that I needed to come stay in the desert at his house, I figured he was up to no good. He never suggested his bright idea to me. He made it seem like some random people were after me. He wanted my mom to convince me to go out there. Popper lived way outside of Los Angeles in the desert – almost two hours' drive. He made statements before: that if gay dudes upset him, he would put them in his trunk, drive them to the desert, kill them, and feed them to the coyotes. He was not going to get me in the middle of nowhere and lie to my mom that I never arrived.

My entire world was coming to a crashing halt. It was hurtful, but I kept pressing on the road to sobriety. I warned all three neighbors in my duplex not to let anyone through the security gate. I felt afraid that my safety was in danger. I was extremely cautious coming in and out of my apartment, and advised my mom to block their numbers. Now for the second time, I had the exact same dream of my bedroom door being kicked in, and I was shot and killed. I experienced the same fright and emotions that I really felt the first time I dreamed this. I knew something was brewing for the worse.

My play nephew, Whiz, was twenty-three years old with a serious drug addiction. He started using meth, and I noticed sores on his arms where he was picking his skin. Often, he would lock himself in my bathroom for hours. He lived with me temporarily, when he got into disagreements with his parents. I really considered him to be like family. I paid to get his haircut and gave him clothes. I did not like anyone to hang around me who was not well groomed. I felt we had a spiritual connection because I was present when he got baptized in Jesus' name, and filled with the Holy Ghost. Apparently, I was wrong. Whiz owed me $40 for the past month. He was avoiding me, but posted photos on social media partying in Las Vegas.

I got upset by the games he was playing. Finally, he answered the phone when I blocked my number. I cursed him out about my money. His friend was in the background saying something sarcastic. Whiz told me to come and pick up my money. I spoke to another gay boy who relayed some lies Whiz said about me. I found it odd because Whiz had gossiped about this same guy to me. As we compared notes, other friends of this guy got upset when I revealed the rumors Whiz said about their crew. It was all a bunch of messy tea (gossip).

The four of us decided to confront Whiz in person at the address he had just given me. He did not know they were coming. I met them at a fast food restaurant, parked my car, and rode with them. I figured I had better grab my hammer because the person in the background sounded irate. Whiz and three other gay boys came outside when we got to the address. We ganged up on Whiz about all the lies he conjured up. It was a scenario of lies and betrayal. We had all been his friends in his moments of despair. He had lived with all of us at different times. All I can speculate is that when he got high, he made up stories to create conversation.

I had the hammer in my waistband. The gay boy Tyrone, who was posing threats in the background started flicking a switchblade in and out. I guess he wanted to intimidate those of us fussing at Whiz. I pulled out my hammer to make a statement to Tyrone. As I was distracted by the verbal altercation with Whiz, I was ambushed by a "sneak attack." Tyrone came up from behind, snatched the hammer, and clobbered me with it. The impact on top of my head from that hammer was so hard, I thought a car hit me. My knees buckled as I collapsed into the street. He proceeded to get on top of me hitting me while I lay there defenseless.

Technically, I was there alone because the people I went with were not my friends. They were acquaintances of Whiz. They did not defend me. One of them said, "Hey, that is still a girl." At some point, he let me up. The hammer dropped, and as soon as I grabbed it he took off running.

Miraculously, I got up with NO INJURIES.
God was on my side!

It seemed to be a set up by Whiz. I planned to cuss him out, pick up my money, and be done with it. I was full of pride. I thought I was invincible. God literally allowed some sense to be knocked into me. He arrested me like the cops say FREEZE, and I surrendered.

SIN had become like an anchor weighing me down.

"Pride goes before destruction, a haughty spirit before a fall."
Proverbs 16:18 (NIV)

I did not go back to my apartment; instead, I called my Uncle Wendell to see if I could stop by. He was out running errands but my auntie was at home. She put some ice on my head where she felt a lump. I wanted to sleep off the devastation. My auntie made me stay up in case I had a concussion.

My friend called to check on me. She told me that there was a video of me being assaulted on Facebook. Somebody else called me suggesting I make a police report. I was embarrassed that this was recorded and circulating on social media. I wanted to handle it myself as they call it 'street justice.' I called G-Main to tell her round up a few of the gang members. She was mad that I went over there alone and did not pick them up before going. My dad begged me to leave it alone and stressed the fact that I was not raised that way. He rushed over to check on me. Dad gave me some much-needed money too. That evening, I went to my house to pack a bag for church. I was skeptical about going to my traditional childhood church in men's clothes. I was extremely emotionally damaged and physically drained.

I was at my lowest point of brokenness.

My desperation outweighed my emotional opposition the Devil tried to use to keep me from going.

The next morning, my quest for freedom began. The pastor was not there but it did not matter. I had an encounter with the King. I did not hesitate at the close of the service to go down the center aisle. I remember my exact outfit. I was wearing a plaid polo button down, cargo pants, and some Air Jordan sneakers. My hair was freshly cut with the sides tapered with deep waves on the top. I walked up to a female minister who knew me since childhood. She did not recognize me right away. When she stared into my face, she realized who I was.

She laid hands on me and the power of God knocked me to the floor. I was crying, speaking in tongues, and repenting. I felt so hot as if there was a presence of fire. I could not keep on the men's button-down shirt. I took it off, a T-shirt was under it. I began to pray on my knees, feeling a release, and a shift take place after travailing a while. I stood up with my hands extended to God feeling thankful for my life. I had an attitude of gratitude after walking away from an assault with a hammer without injury. I found out later my Aunt Lynette was taking pictures and forwarding them to my mom.

"This poor man cried, and the LORD heard him, and saved him out of all his troubles." Psalm 34:6 (KJV)

December 14, 2014, was the day my life began to change.

I started staying at my Uncle Wendell's house on a regular basis deliberately avoiding the drug customers who stopped by without notice yelling, "Esko" from downstairs. My house had been the hangout for many years. I would stop by to check my mail every few days and my neighbors would notify me of any disturbances. I was steering clear of my residence for a while.

I returned to my childhood church for about four Sundays. Those who remembered me as a little girl were glad to see me. Surprisingly, nobody harassed me about wearing men's street clothes. The pastor was ill for over a month, so he was absent. After all those years I saw Minister Berry at communion, and he gave me a big hug. Finally, Pastor returned. It was heartwarming to see him feeling better. He was like a spiritual father to me growing up. I videotaped a segment of him singing, and posted it on social media. A church employee got upset and equated me to the person who filmed Whitney Houston in her casket. Ironically, I was at the club when the Icon sang in Hollywood a few days before she was found dead in the bathtub. I was highly offended by that remark. I realized that the Jezebel spirit of control, intimidation, and manipulation was still prevalent through the powers that be. I politely left the church that I was raised in once again. This time, I was determined not to allow any situation to be a stumbling block and cause me to fall from grace.

I visited Bishop Noel Jones' church over the years and always brought in my New Year's Eve there before making a commitment to Christ. I decided to join, spending 6 hours one Saturday in a seminar for new members. My mom had a friend who was an evangelist at this church. When I was a teen, she prophesied to me that I was an evangelist. She was an instructor in the new members class. During the coffee break, I approached her. She remembered me, and I told her I had rededicated my life to the Lord. She was nice and very happy to see me on the right path. However, I had not considered coming out of men's clothes yet. I explained to her that I had no other clothes to wear. She volunteered to give me some women's apparel.

A week later, my cousin Calvin "the movie star" text me one night inviting me to hang out in Hollywood Hills. He had spiraled downward abusing drugs and alcohol after a rough divorce. Chili, a male associate, and I drove up there. The house was located on a cliff overlooking the city. I did not see a space to park so I blocked someone's driveway. I text Calvin, he did not reply, and when I called, there was no answer. I was hoping that I did not drive 20 minutes up the winding road on a dry run. Five minutes later, he walked up to the car. I got out to greet him, but when I turned to tell my friends to get out, he vanished. We were trying to figure out which house he entered. The screen door was open so I heard his voice echoing outside. I walked in and Calvin introduced me as his cousin. My friends announced their names. There were four other guests there already and Calvin was acting weird and fidgety. It dawned on me that my car was blocking the neighbors' driveway.

"Hey, can I pull up here?" I asked.

The owner of the home was acting antsy.

"Let me show you where to park," the homeowner said.

When we walked outside, I noticed a black BMW with tinted windows parked by the cliff. The fog lights were on so I knew someone was inside the car. The guy directed me to double-park blocking his carport. The BMW pulled up and parked behind me. I guess Calvin recognized that car from the surveillance camera. I re-entered the home.

"Cousin, I am going to come stay at your place tonight," he said.

"Okay, that's fine," I said.

"Great, let's go," Calvin said, anxiously.

I did not understand why I had just moved my car for us to leave in such a hurry. We all exited in a group and Calvin was the last to walk out. The person in the black BMW got out of the car and I proceeded to get into my car. Then I heard a commotion. I looked out of my rear-view mirror to see Calvin sucker punched by the dude. My male friend got out attempting to get involved. A gun fell to the ground. Another dude was sitting in that black BMW as well.

"Calvin, let's go. Come on," I yelled, adamantly.

My friend tried to guide him toward the car, but Calvin was so uncontrollable that he threw his cell phone.

"I am not leaving until this guy gives me another round fighting," Calvin said, demandingly.

I left him there once he refused to leave. We could have all gotten shot and thrown off that cliff. I called my mom and my Aunt Lynette to tell them what happened. If I did not go up there that night I don't know how that would have turned out for Calvin. I believe the altercation did not escalate, because they knew his family had just left and could trace any foul play back to that residence. He called the next day convinced that his phone was in my backseat, even though he never made it to my car. We have not spoken since.

After God spared me once again from a dangerous situation, I knew I had to make some permanent changes. I went home and flushed all the cocaine down the toilet. I put all the paraphernalia in the trash outside. I was still on the '21 days to break a habit' campaign. I did not vacillate getting rid of the drugs first. My intentions were to ease my way out by selling it and retire from the drug game. That would have been a repeated cycle of never stopping because of greed. I had to take a leap of faith. I decided to live for Christ no matter what I had to give up.

"Do not worry about tomorrow, for tomorrow will worry about itself."
Matthew 6:34a (NIV)

Within a few days, I changed my phone number. I was not interested in hearing any more gossip. I knew my phone was going to be blowing up from the video of me getting attacked with the hammer. I just desired peace after months of being the hot topic in the "gay press." The two main doors I shut right away were temptation and communication. I did not want to risk

getting high or being enticed back into my familiar gay circle. The Word of God says, *"Be not deceived: Evil communications corrupt good manners. Come out from among them and be separate"*
(1 Corinthians 15:33, 2 Corinthians 6:17a KJV).

I had given G-Main my new number not even thinking. I considered her to be like family because she was my nephew Jeckle's' best friend. She asked twice where the assault with the hammer took place. I no longer wanted to retaliate. She became persistent as I reiterated that I was leaving it in God's hands. It was tempting to consent to the proposition. My feelings were still hurt from the attack, but I knew guilt would eat me up. When she left my house, I literally cried praying aloud, "The Bible declares that vengeance is Mine saith the Lord; I will repay, and if it is true show me personally God."

Bishop Noel Jones' messages of reconciliation were mending the wounds that I suffered from for years. I felt as if I had exhausted all my options. God had left me no other choice besides serving Him. In the beginning, the devil was making me feel afraid of the future to the point that I was not content. One Wednesday night, I got a revelation in bible study. After weeks of Bishop Jones' preaching on Ephesians 1, the eyes of my understanding were enlightened.
"Serving God should not be laborious," Bishop Jones said.

I busted into laughter and felt the joy of the Lord come over me. From that night on I was happily content serving the Lord. I was so blessed to sit under a ministry mogul with such knowledge of the word. My new pastor, Bishop Jones helped me get through a rough time of transition. Being in a diverse church with no stern stipulations caused me to attend without feeling displaced.

The church was huge and several gay people I personally knew attended the 11:00a.m. service. I was determined to avoid them, so I switched to the 8:00 a.m. service. The gays were not up that early after clubbing on Saturday night. The worship music had me in tears while sitting in church. God was breaking up the fallow ground and replacing it with a heart of flesh. It seemed as if I was crying through the entire service.

I began attending the Sunday night service. The evangelist had given me a huge bag of women's clothes a few weeks after our conversation. She had become a spiritual mother to me. Sometimes, my friend Chili would join me at church. She was Catholic, but she liked Bishop Noel Jones' articulate delivery of the Word. Chili was one of the few friends left after all the "conflama" (drama and conflict). I started having a gut instinct that my life was in jeopardy. Chili told me the newest rumor was that I went to jail and became an informant. Truth be told, I had never been arrested. It had to be God who kept my record clear.

My auntie had weight-loss surgery so the food they ate was healthy. After about a month, I started staying at my apartment some nights. I liked to cook fattening food. Chili lived four blocks away from me. We hung out daily since my fast life was changing. She smoked marijuana, but stopped because she was applying for a management position at her job. We ate dinner together a few nights of the week.

One night we were hanging out at my house when my mom called. We both conversed with her on the speakerphone. Chili even reiterated to my mom the drama that transpired along with the rumors. Chili began to ask my mom some questions about the Bible. My mom answered her questions but then said, "Shonda, do you want to receive the Holy Ghost?" Shonda was her real name. I thought to myself that my mom was being ridiculous. All she asked was a few questions about the Bible.
"Yes, I do want it," she said.
I was completely speechless.
"Get the oil and anoint her head," Mom said.
I anointed Chili's head with the oil. My mother began to pray and told Chili to start praising God by saying, "Hallelujah Jesus." Shonda aka Chili got filled with the Holy Ghost. She was speaking in tongues on my couch for almost an hour that night.

My Last B-day Bash

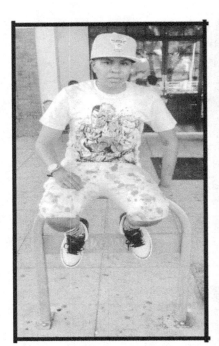

@Beverly Hills Condo(sex traffickers)

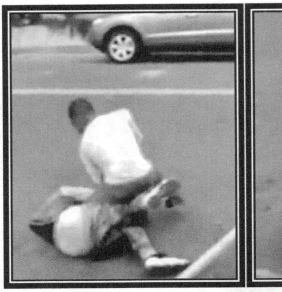

Hammer Attack-God sent a warrant out in the Spirit for my arrest

Dec. 14, 2014 My Life Began to Change

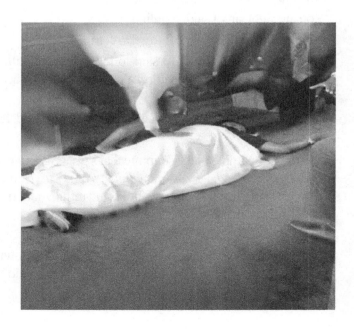

He Ordered My Steps

The devil was relentless. He was tempting me to go to Las Vegas Gay Pride. All the people I had conflicts with would be there. That demonic suggestion made no sense. I would have to keep my presence unknown if I went, but I did not want to miss the excitement. I contemplated going, so I was making minor arrangements. I got a haircut and laid out a few outfits on my bed. The devil was telling me, "Have one last party."

My mom called shortly after I entertained the thought. "Hey what are you up to?" she asked, in an investigative tone.

"Oh, just here at home," I said, misleadingly.

"Prophet Mac is on the phone; he wanted to check on you. He thinks you might have some plans," she said, inquiringly.

"Hi, how are you? The Lord showed me that you are trying to go somewhere that you shouldn't," he said.

"You are right sir," I said, giggling.

God had pulled the cover off my secret trip.

"It is not worth it. The Lord said to tell you to be still. Do not allow the Enemy to get you in his territory. You are in a safe place walking with the Lord," he said, with concern.

"Amen, that is so true, sir. I am glad you called," I said, humbly.

It is a prime example of the scripture that says, *"Submit yourselves therefore to God. Resist the devil, and he will flee from you"* (James 4:7 KJV). I was the type of person who was wild, bold, and influential in my sinful life. Satan did not want to lose one of his best representatives.

March 2015, was my last men's haircut. I started allowing my hairline to grow in from that boxed defined lineup. I knew it would be rough but I was willing to endure the afro stages of looking shabby. I was dreading the transition back into a woman. I even tried to bargain with God that if I stopped doing everything else could I, at least, stay in the men's clothes. The Bible answered that for me.

"A woman must not wear men's clothing, nor a man wear women's clothing, for the Lord your God detests anyone who does this." Deuteronomy 22:5 (NIV)

One Sunday night, I arrived at the evening service early at City of Refuge pastored by Bishop Noel Jones. I had become accustomed to attending church on a regular basis now. It was April 2015, I parked in the lot on the church's premises. A minister at the church was getting out of his vehicle at the same time. I felt compelled to ask him for prayer. He grabbed both of my hands in the parking lot. He began to prophesy about the calling on my life. Tears streamed down my face. I thought I had forfeited my opportunity for ministry twenty years ago.

An estimation of about two hundred people came back to this mega church at night. When I got inside, I had an entire section to myself. The worship team was singing a beautiful song as I stood with my eyes closed and arms extended. I heard a whisper, "Do not come back in here with those clothes on." I opened my eyes and looked around but no one was near me. I heard it again, then I knew the Lord was admonishing me to change my appearance. I got home from the church, and immediately began to try on the clothes that the evangelist had given me. That bag had sat on my couch for a month. I was astonished by the way everything fit. Some of the items still had the price tags on them.

I asked myself, "How are you going to wear these clothes without dress shoes? Furthermore, your hair is a mess." I had no clue then how my journey would unfold, but I trusted God.
"Now faith is confidence in what we hope for and assurance about what we do not see" (Hebrews 11:1 NIV).

I battled with anxiety attacks. The idea of transitioning was tormenting my mind. The devil was telling me I would look like a 'drag queen.' I knew in my heart that I was doing the right thing. Satan has been a liar since the beginning of time. I was born a woman, it was impossible for me to look like a drag queen. I was becoming who God created me to be.

I ignored G-Main's phone calls. She tricked me and used somebody else's phone. The devil was attempting to use her to get me to backslide.

"Big dog, what's up Blood? We trying to spend some money," this person said.

"Who is this?" I asked.

The phone got passed to G-Main.

"What's the deal Blood? Let's turn up, Esko," G-Main said.

"I am out of bounds right now, far from home so I cannot meet with y'all tonight," I said.

"Well what time are you coming back tonight?" she asked.

"I'm not, but hey let me catch this other call," I said, hurriedly.

Something seemed strange. They were too pushy asking so many questions. Once I hung up I was uneasy about her strategy to contact me. They claimed to want $60 worth of cocaine, and said they had alcohol. That was very rare with those two because they always wanted a deal on a $20 bag. Instead of being the usual leeches, they had money, marijuana, and a bottle of alcohol.

A week later, G-Main called again, but from a gang member named Frog's phone. He was from Swan Bloods too. I had his number stored in my phone as a customer. I did not answer at first. He sent a text asking if he could pick something up from me. I did not reply so he called back. When I picked up the phone it was silent. They accidentally pocket-dialed me.

"Hello hello," I said.

I heard Frog and G-Main talking about me.

"Esko turned on us working undercover with the cops. People get killed like that blood," Frog said.

I heard G-Main agree with him. I was concluding that Keisha poisoned them with lies. Keisha was relentless in her misery. That was not cool for her to put that label on me. The street rules are "snitches get stitches." Now the gang members were thinking I was an informant. God allowed me to hear another plot against me. I knew then my discernment was accurate on all my inclinations. Everyone seemed to be disgruntled like a chain reaction.

I called a prayer line nightly. A prophet from Jamaica hosted the call Monday through Friday. It started at midnight. I looked forward to getting on this line to hear him pray. He had a thunderous theatrical voice. My mom and two aunts had been calling the line for the past year. Chili and I would sit in the car and listen to the prayer line some nights. I was looking for an apartment because I did not want to reside where I was anymore. Prophet Hunter told me to go east. I started looking in Paramount, Ca. My Aunt Lona dropped some money off to me for food and gas. She had always been a blessing down through the years.

I took some anointed oil and went through my house praying with it. I went in my stairway and put oil on the handrail and security gate. I got so radical, I even went out on the sidewalk pouring oil. I walked to the corner drizzling oil there.

"I command angels to dispatch on the four corners of my premises. Lord, keep any evil spirit off my street and let me have peace where I live in name of Jesus," I said.

"For the weapons of our warfare are not carnal, but mighty through God to the pulling down of strongholds" (2 Corinthians 10:4 KJV).

My mom's other friend prophetess Shannon called me. She was so excited that I was striving to get my life together. She invited me to her church and said she wanted to bless me with some money. I met her at Bethlehem Temple, off 52nd and McKinley. She gave me $50 dollars. That was a blessing during the time I sacrificed fast money for salvation. They showed me a lot of love, and Pastor Richardson was very encouraging. My cousin

Dayna took me down for prayer. The ministerial team surrounded me, smearing anointed oil all over me. Both my arms, my head and even the tip of my tennis shoes were shining when they finished. I needed all the prayer I could get on this journey.

Mother's Day weekend 2014, I took that money to buy a wig at the beauty supply. I was not sure what kind of style would be suitable for me. Usually, the Koreans were quick to say you look nice as a tactic for you to spend money. However, the devil used the clerk to laugh hysterically at everything I tried on. I got discouragingly frustrated, so I called my mom. She suggested I send her pictures so we could decide together. I finally bought a wig and a dollar lipstick. Payless shoe store was in the same shopping center. I went and purchased a pair of two-inch pumps that I called "Lil Debbie's."

I drove to my Uncle Wendell's house. He and my aunt watched me try the wig on and loved it. I called my mom on the video chat. She was surprised at how pretty I looked. It had been so long since she saw me display any feminine characteristics. That was one of the best Mother's Day blessings she had experienced in a long time. Money could not buy the joy she felt seeing her daughter coming back into alignment with God's Word.

I went to the 11 o'clock Sunday service on Mother's Day. I was paranoid that my neighbors would see me coming out of my apartment. I felt like I was wearing a disguise. I was ushered to a seat beside a stud; I knew right away that she was a woman because her breasts were large. Her temperament was so restless that she got up ten minutes later and never returned. I had such a great time praising God that day. It was a freedom in my worship knowing that I had obeyed God. After service, I went to find the minister who prayed for me in the parking lot. He was so proud of me and told me I looked beautiful. Another minister whose marriage seminars I attended some Tuesdays was rejoicing with me too. I went back over to Bethlehem Temple that same day. Pastor Gentry Richardson came out into the audience and kissed my cheek.

"Your latter will be greater than your past," Pastor Richardson said.

I felt the power of God in that declaration.

The Great Escape

Talking to my mom on the phone for hours was a new hobby. She was used to me always being in such a rush, but now my new life did not consist of much activity. I would even text her addresses to Google apartments. I was looking to move real soon so I wanted to show her my potential residences.

"I have a room for you here," my mom kept saying. I would get annoyed whenever she suggested. I had no interest in relocating. Although she was blessed to be the first tenant in brand new two bedrooms. I was not considering joining her. I did not want to leave Southern California at all.

I was beginning to adopt an abstinent lifestyle of holiness. Being sober and committed to my "21 days to break a habit" made it easier. Cigarettes, marijuana, alcohol, and cocaine had been taken off my "things to do list." I was seeking the Lord diligently and laid prostrate beside my bed on the carpet praying daily. I spoke in tongues for hours, sometimes falling asleep without realizing it.

I was desperate for deliverance. All these years what appeared to look good on the outside was a diabolical plot. Searching and obsessing for something that never completely satisfied me was over. God was the only healing balm for my emotional scars.

"In the same way, the Spirit helps us in our weakness. We do not know what we ought to pray for, but the Spirit himself intercedes for us through wordless groans." Romans 8:26 (NIV)

One evening toward the end of May, the phone rang. I picked up.
"Hi, mom."

"Hey baby, I got my friend Prophet Mac on a three-way with us. He wants to tell you something," she said.

"Hi, how are you?" he asked, very pleasantly.

"I am okay," I said, very skeptically.

"Woman of God," he said, with an authoritative posture. I thought he was talking to my mom.

He said again, "Woman of God."

"Yes sir," I replied, hesitating as my heart raced.

I felt awkward as I sat in men's clothes and he was calling me something I did not look like. The Holy Ghost in me stood at attention though.

"Make haste, there is a hit out on your life. God said to tell you if you stay under the umbrella of safety, He has you covered. I'm looking at you in a vision packing a suitcase boarding an airplane. (He started speaking in tongues powerfully). God has everything mapped out like how a director films the end of a movie first. You just obey God!" he said, sternly.

"Yes sir, thank you so much for that warning. I felt my life is in jeopardy too. I told my mom the same people who are acting concerned are in on it," I said, relieved of the paranoid feeling.

I was staying clear of past acquaintances and continuing to focus on Jesus for direction. That was truly the confirmation my mom needed to hear. Those former long-term friends who called her were conspiring liars. God was watching out for me in every aspect. I knew instantly that prophetic word meant I was supposed to be relocating with my mom.

For some reason, I just could not wrap my natural mind around moving out of the state of California. I loved Los Angeles. My mom always referred to her recent location as, "this lil city." The way she made it seem, I thought there were dirt roads. I knew there was an urgency to move somewhere without second guessing. I was hoping to find an apartment in a city outside of Los Angeles. I was thinking at the time, maybe the cities of: Paramount, Victorville, Valencia, or Anaheim California.

Frequently, I watched TBN Christian television. I stayed barricaded back in my room living in fear. I had a 40-watt lamp that I used instead of my ceiling light. My apartment was on the corner of a residential street. You could see my living room window driving down Crenshaw Boulevard. Aside from going to church, I would not leave my house. I kept all the lights off to avoid the constant lurkers. Joel Osteen came on talking about Joseph and used the exact analogy that Prophet Mac did. "Our lives are already orchestrated like the end of a movie is filmed first," Osteen said. I could not believe how the Lord kept encouraging me that my life had a bright future.

One day, I had come from my bedroom located at the back of my house. As I walked around the corner approaching my kitchen I thought to myself, 'being in the house getting groceries for the month is not so bad.' The Holy Spirit replied to my thought, "I came that you might have life and life more abundantly. This is not living." My mindset shifted that very moment. I accepted the fact that moving needed to be a priority so I no longer had to hide. The devil was trying to keep me living in fear. I was not hiding when I looked like a boy gallivanting around town, so why would I go under the radar now.

God's Word describes, *"For God hath not given us the spirit of fear; but of power, and of love, and of a sound mind."* 2 Timothy 1:7 (KJV)

I turned on TBN, and one of my favorite pastors was preaching. At the very moment, I tuned in he was screaming, "Make haste, make haste, make haste, make haste!" The tone of his voice was ground shaking. The hair on my arms stood up. The anointing was all over me manifested in goose bumps. Bishop T.D. Jakes gave the confirmation that I needed to move out of the state of California.

I had no money, and I wondered how I was going to get out of here. I did not see the need to pack up 4 closets full of men's clothes. I owned close to a hundred pairs of shoes rowed around the walls in their boxes. I knew my transition into women's attire was approaching. I began to pull all the clothes out of the closets and piled them on my sectional couch. I was just given new furniture passed down six months prior from a gay boy I called my daughter. I was taking nothing on my journey. Those spirits attached to all my possessions were going to disconnect from me. I spent the entire afternoon dragging that stuff to the front. My living room was cluttered with barely any space to maneuver around it.

Femininity was knocking at the door of my heart.

I was having separation anxiety as I bagged up my things. The devil was telling me that I was crazy to get rid of all my costly urban street wear. Some of those Jordan tennis shoes, I stood in line to buy before the stores opened. Chili had stopped by and saw how serious I was about discarding of my belongings. She suggested selling them on the internet. Time was ticking, and I did not want to spend months negotiating piece by piece online.

Chili worked with all men on her job. She asked some of the fellas if they knew who bought clothes and tennis shoes. Chili called me from her job and told me the addresses of two places that I could sell my wardrobe. I procrastinated for a week conditioning my mind to muster up the energy to "just go ahead and do it."

A fresh start included opposition, which is all a part of warfare. The devil knew if I stayed in those clothes, he could subtly draw me back into perversion. Furthermore, how could the glory of God be seen if no one recognized a change? I could attempt to convince a stranger that I was a Christian, but my appearance would lead them to the assumption of sincere deception.

"Therefore, if any man be in Christ, he is a new creature: old things are passed away; behold, all things are become new" (2 Corinthians 5:17 KJV).

One afternoon I walked across to the mall where I parked my car remaining incognito. I pulled in front of my apartment to fill my trunk, front, and back seat with clothes. I drove toward Hollywood on La Brea and 3rd to a consignment shop. I got a basket from inside and made a few trips getting everything. I negotiated each item. The guy was trying to auction low.

"Listen man, I need all the cash you can give me. I am starting a new life with Christ. I will not be wearing these clothes. God is taking me in a different direction. I am moving out of state." I said.

I went in my phone showing him the one photo of myself dressed as a woman from Mother's Day. He looked surprised.

Finally, he said, "That's awesome. I am going to give you the top pay for these items. They are in great condition. I was trying to go low so we could get more profit reselling them, but I got you don't worry," He smiled.

"Thank you, I appreciate that," I said.

What he was initially trying to give me $2 per item for increased to between $8-13. I left that store with close to a thousand dollars. I took a huge cut compared to the thousands of dollars I spent on my wardrobe. God had a new journey for me. I was so grateful for the provision to buy an airplane ticket.

I was always on the phone with my mom and Auntie Neecy. I called my mom and said, "I did it Mom. God is so good. I got close to a thousand for those clothes."

"Wow, thank you Jesus!" she said, excitedly. "Hold on. I got your auntie on the line, let me merge her in."

"Hey Auntie, I sold the clothes," I said, in a bubbly tone.

"Hey, now God can move," she said, joyfully.

I felt a quickening jolt hit my body. The power of God was on that statement. He was on the move from that day forward.

My Aunties' Neecy and Von were coming to visit California. My uncle Wendell had a BBQ every 4th of July. I was anticipating seeing them for the holiday weekend. This would be the first year that I would not be attending Los Angeles Gay Pride. I began to check the airfare for after the holiday. I was thinking possibly July 11th, a week after my family gathering. There was a certain flight the Holy Ghost said, "Book it."

Being filled with God's Spirit with the evidence of speaking in other tongues, you receive instructions through a still small voice. *"When the Spirit of truth comes, he will guide you into all truth. He will not speak on his own but will tell you what he has heard. He will tell you about the future."* John 16:13 (NLT)

Leaning to my own understanding, I was challenging God's instructions by looking at the price. This one-way ticket was $400. I had taken round trips cheaper than that on many occasions. It was peak season in June. The departure date was June 15th. That meant I would be gone before my family cookout. I compared the rates after the 4th of July. A one-way ticket, three days after the holiday was only $150 – a huge difference. Worse yet, there were two layovers if I booked the $400 ticket. The odds did not make sense to me. I felt stressed out. I kept the website up on my laptop and took a break to make lunch. Once I resumed my search, the Holy Ghost said again, "Book that flight!"

I started thinking about how the crime rate in Los Angeles escalated during the 4th of July. Many drive by shootings transpired because gunshots could be easily mistaken for fireworks. Within me, I felt very strongly that if I stayed behind I was not going to make it out alive. I disregarded my own logic and adhered to the voice of God. I booked that ticket for June 15th leaving the LAX Airport at 10:00 a.m. I was scheduled to arrive in Michigan after midnight.

I took my tennis shoes to an athletic store downtown that Chili referred. I had only worn each shoe less than five times. The bottom of the shoes was not even dirty. The guy inspected them closely. They only bought Jordan's and wanted 25 pairs out of the 40 I had because they were only interested in special editions. That still worked for me. They wrote me a check for $1,100.

Chili asked if I wanted to sell my car. I had not given it any thought. My plans were to park it in my uncle Wendell's garage.

"I can buy it in about two weeks when I get paid depending on what you're asking for it," Chili said.

"Well, I would like $2,500. I might get more for online. Koreans love to buy Hondas," I said.

"Sure, once I get my next paycheck I would love to purchase it," Chili said.

"Okay, if that's past the calendar date of my departure, I will leave the pink slip with my uncle. You can deposit the money into my account," I said.

I was tired of the LGBTQ culture taking me in circles. Some disconnections can bless your life. Even the ones who betrayed me were a part of God's divine plan. At the point that I submitted and committed myself unto the Lord, He began to do a NEW thing.

I was counting down the days until my move. I continued to call the prayer line faithfully every night. I did not feel as nervous as I did before. My trust in God's protection kept me grounded. Isaiah 54:17 says, *"No weapon formed against you shall prosper."* I was trying to figure out what I was taking on my trip. I had thirteen pairs of shoes that could be worn as a woman. A few of them were Doc Marten boots in bright colors. I had some tennis shoes that did not look masculine and bulky.

I gathered T-shirts, basketball shorts, a few jeans, and sweatpants in a pile to pack. I walked past these items to glance out my living room window. The Holy Ghost said, "You will not need all that stuff where I am taking you." I turned around to observe all the items that I planned to take. I decided what was not necessary. At least, I wanted to have something to put on while lounging around the house. I knew I would probably rest a few days once I got there. I wore men's underwear so I packed enough for a week. I was going to buy bras and panties, along with women's clothing when I got settled in my new city.

Two more weeks passed, and Chili called.

"I need more time some bills are due," she said.

"Oh, well when do you think you can buy my car?" I asked.

"I'm getting a check in three days out of my 401k," Chili said.

"Oh perfect," I replied.

Another week had gone by, and Chili still seemed to be gathering up her money.

My cousin Pooh called.

"Hey girl, I heard you are moving. What are you doing with your car? I just got $5,000 on my direct deposit card. I have no idea where this money mysteriously appeared from," Pooh said, happily.

"Oh wow, Chili was supposed to buy it. I'm going to give her until Friday. If she does not produce the money, the car is yours to buy," I said, assuredly.

"Alright cousin, keep me posted. Anyway, I am going to stop by to say goodbye before you go. I will talk to you later," Pooh said.

"Alright, I will let you know the verdict; see you soon bye bye."

On June 14, 2015, I received a call from a lawyer's office.

"Hi Miss Collins; I'm calling to tell you there is a check here for you," the receptionist said.

"Oh ok, I will be there shortly," I said, surprised.

My car had been rear ended twice in 2014. I was already compensated for the first accident. I got paid unexpectedly on the second car wreck. There is an old song that says, "He's an on-time God. Yes, He is. He may not come when you want Him, but He will be there right on time." I had a one-thousand-dollar check given to me the day before I boarded the plane. I could not believe how quickly God allowed me to have $3,000.

He is a rewarder of those who diligently seek Him. Hebrews 11:6b (KJV)

I was given a huge new suitcase that stood on four wheels with a retractable handle. After sorting through my stuff, everything fit right in there. I was anxious to go at that point. I abandoned my furnished apartment. I just had bought a $2,000 bed less than a year ago, but I had no time to try and auction off furniture or electronics. Not to mention the several remaining pairs of shoes that the consignment shop did not buy. I was chalking up my losses like when Jesus told the rich man leave all you have to follow me. I was saying goodbye to my familiar surroundings – it was bittersweet. I loved LA, but I knew this obedient act of faith was beneficial.

My Uncle Wendell was taking me to the airport. I drove over to his house early that morning. My uncle's wife was such a sweetheart.

"Bye Auntie, love you. I will surely miss you guys," I said.

"Love you too, make sure you don't forget about us," she replied.

My uncle put my suitcase in the back of his pickup truck, and we headed to the airport. Once I arrived curbside at the airport it got real. My eyes were swollen with tears.

"I love you Uncle, thank you for everything," I said.

"Love you too baby," he replied, as he hugged me.

He got my suitcase from the back. I checked it in with the skycap. My boarding pass was already printed, so I went directly to the security checkpoint.

I felt in my spirit that this was "the dawning of a new day."

I looked androgynous, which is partly male and partly female in appearance; of indeterminate sex. I had a manicure, pedicure, and brow waxing a few days before my trip. My nails were polished electric purple, my eyebrows were arched to perfection, and I had a tiny afro with men's clothes on. My hair had sprouted out a little bit from March until June.

The first layover was in Phoenix, Arizona. That flight took about an hour.

"All passengers going to Chicago may remain seated. We are letting off some passengers and boarding others," the flight attendant announced on the intercom.

I was not certain if I should get off because my next layover was in Chicago.

"Ma'am, excuse me my next layover is in Chicago. Am I supposed to board another plane to get there?" I asked.

"Let me see your ticket," she responded.

"No. you are supposed to stay on this plane, but you are more than welcome to move closer to the front of the cabin," the flight attendant replied.

"Thank you so much," I said.

I grabbed my carry-on from the overhead and sat by a window toward the front. I was scrolling through social media as we waited for new passengers to board.

"Get off your phone and watch the people. I will have someone on this plane to speak a word to you," the Holy Ghost said to me. The best way I can describe it is an intuition. The Holy Ghost is like the sixth sense to a believer in Christ. The scripture says, *"Whoever has ears, let them hear what the Spirit says"* (Revelation 2:7a NIV).

I became attentive. Everyone was rushing on the airplane to find seats. I noticed a Caucasian woman dressed like those from the United Pentecostal sect. Her hair was in a bun on the top of her head; her long sleeve floral top was buttoned up to her neck, and her skirt was down to the floor. Soon as I thought that could be the person, two other ladies came behind her dressed exactly like she was, and with buns on top of their heads. I knew they would all be sitting together. A few more people boarded the aircraft.

A man took the aisle seat on my row, which left the middle seat vacant. An older African American woman boarded. I was wondering if she was the person. I noticed images of dollar bills plastered on the front of her T-shirt. I thought, 'no, that is not her because she has on a rapper's shirt.' We made eye contact as she walked past. I looked over my shoulder and in that split second, she turned around.

"Excuse me, is that seat available?" she asked.

"Yes ma'am, it is empty," I said.

"Oh ok, excuse me," she said, to the man seated in the aisle.

"Hi, my name is Ms. Lake.

"Nice to meet you ma'am, I am Nichol."

After take-off, Ms. Lake began to converse with me.

"I am going to Rochester, New York to see my daughter," she said.

"Oh, how nice, my destination is Detroit Michigan," I said.

"Yes, I'm from New York, but I'm helping my son and his wife with my grandchildren in Phoenix. I've been living here since my other son was murdered in Rochester," she said.

"Sorry to hear that. I hear Phoenix is scorching hot this time of year," I said.

"Sure is," Ms. Lake laughed.

"Well, I am moving from Los Angeles. I lived another life that was not glorifying God. I had a rough year in 2014," I said.

"The Lord says to let you know that the peace you are looking for will be found when your feet touch the pavement. The people who set you up, you are going to hear about their demise" she said, prophetically.

"I know flesh and blood could not have revealed that to you ma'am. I got assaulted by a guy with a hammer," I said.

"My God, that's awful. The Lord loves you dearly," she said.

The presence of God was resting between us on that aircraft. Tears rolled down my face. I was speaking in tongues in a low whisper. I was lost for words staring out the window into the heavens. Later, Ms. Lake pointed to her T-shirt referring to a famous boxer she was related to. The dollar signs represented his boxing name Money Mayweather. I treated her to dinner during our layover in Chicago. I walked Ms. Lake to her gate to board the next plane to New York. I had about another hour before my next flight. I sat at a charging station and called to tell my mom what took place.

When I landed in Detroit there was a sense of relief as I exhaled. I knew my safety was no longer an issue. I waited at baggage claims for my suitcase and proceeded to stand on the curbside elated to see my mother. She jumped out of the car to embrace me.

"You are safe," she said.

I just cried tears of joy. We sat in the car in silence for at least two minutes before driving off.

"You are glowing. I can see the peace of God upon you," Mom said.

"It's the dawning of a new day," I said, cheerfully.

Three days after I arrived, my cousin Pooh bought my car. She deposited the money in my account and picked the car up from my uncle's house. Chili and I did not keep in contact once I told her that the car was sold. I had close to $5,000 to get a good jump start with my women's wardrobe. I even had to purchase panties after wearing men's underwear for twenty years. I wanted to go to restaurants, parks and get acquainted with my new city. I was glad to be liberated after all the confinement to my apartment for months in Los Angeles.

Started growing my hair and regularly attending church

Mother's Day 2015 1st time as a woman in many years w/Aunt Lona

Caterpillar2 Butterfly

Metamorphosis is a change of the form or nature of a thing or person into a completely different one, by natural or supernatural means. My deliverance was a TRANSFORMATION process. I made extreme changes in my learned behavior and appearance. Perversion is a stronghold in itself, and I had so many things that I needed to be freed from.

Confession is the first step in admitting who you are in order to overcome.

Honesty was very important going through my deliverance stages. I had to be honest with God as well as myself. The Enemy will thrive on darkness. I had to acknowledge that I needed deliverance.

"The TRUTH will make you FREE" John 8:32b (KJV)

I had to get rid of pride. "God opposes the proud, but gives grace to the humble." (James 4:6 NLT). Recognizing that my dependency was on Jesus and His provisions for deliverance, my heart was in a state of repentance. My mind was determined to turn away from sin and Satan. I was willing to turn from everything that hindered my spiritual growth.

I completed some renunciations aloud. Renouncing is an action resulting from repentance. It is forsaking all evil making a clean break from Satan and all his works. I verbally broke agreement with the sins I had previously engaged in. I served Satan an eviction notice.

"I renounce my involvement in all sexual sin including: perversion, adultery, masturbation, fornication, fantasy, pornography, and homosexuality in the name of Jesus. I renounce and break agreement with all ungodly soul ties with sexual partners in the name of Jesus. I loose myself from succubus and incubus spirits (demons that have sex with people in their sleep) in the name of Jesus. I renounce every spirit of addiction to drugs and alcohol; I command it to come out of my appetite in the name of Jesus. I command all spirits of lust and sexual addictions that work with witchcraft to leave in the name of Jesus. I forgive any person that has ever rejected, mishandled, offended, hurt, or abused me in the name of Jesus" I pronounced, with authority.

God forgives us of our trespasses, so He expects us to forgive those who have mistreated us. Forgiveness was essential to my deliverance. If you never get an apology, you want to forgive to be free. *"For if you forgive men their trespasses, your heavenly Father will also forgive you."* Matthew 6:14 (NKJV)

I was fasting three days out of the week for six months straight. Monday, Wednesday, and Friday from midnight until 4:00 p.m. I constantly read my Bible, listened to worship music, and prayed in tongues. Those measures of commitment began to renew my mind. I prayed for over an hour sometimes falling asleep while I spoke in tongues. The Holy Spirit makes intercession praying according to God's will. That is the heavenly language of communication that the devil cannot decode.

"Jesus said, *'This kind can come forth by nothing, but by prayer and FASTING"* Mark 9:29 (KJV).

After 7 months of my lifestyle shift, I permanently changed my wardrobe. Despite my discomfort in women's clothes that I was not used to wearing, I kept pressing forward. The devil made jokes in my mind. His "drag queen" accusations were redundant. I had to block them out and stick to my decision to serve the Lord.

I got re-baptized in the name of JESUS for my "conscience sake." Since I had not been baptized since childhood, I felt it was necessary to escape any condemnation of my past transgressions. I eliminated any room for the devil to make me feel dirty or unworthy. I was washed, covered, and sealed by the Blood of Jesus through a liquid form of cleansing. Covered means to be protected, and sealed is to be made definite.

After about a year, I genuinely embraced womanhood. I looked forward to shopping, different hairstyles, and nail polish. Yet, I battled with a sense of shame, guilt, and failure. I was afraid to tell anyone about my past life as a transgender. I thought no one would want to be around me. I turned on TBN one evening.

"He who the Son sets free is free indeed!" Bishop T.D. Jakes yelled, those words while preaching.

My spirit quickened; I leaped off my couch, running, and speaking in tongues. The weight of condemnation lifted off me that day. I have been sharing my story of deliverance ever since.

I discovered Whiz had a stroke at twenty-three years old. He is the one I called my nephew that set me up when I got hit with the hammer. Then the gay guy Richie was murdered shortly after I heard about Whiz. He was the one who robbed me, and then left me in that smoldering hot car passed out drunk; insisting I gave him my drugs and money. I saw a post on social media involving the people who leaked the sex tape. One of them was badly beaten up twice, and the other one went to jail.

I reached out to Whiz, and he gave a genuine apology via social media. A week later, he text my mom asking her to forgive him. I felt bad for them, but the Lord brought back to my remembrance what I had prayed. God's Word cannot return void. *"Vengeance is mine; I will repay says the Lord"* (Romans 12:19 NKJV). The only reason God spared Whiz's life is that he was saved. The woman on that airplane Ms. Lake prophesied that I would hear of my enemies' demise.

I will tell my testimony as long as I am breathing. Half of the world is consumed by homosexuality. I asked God, "Get this out of me, or get me out of this." We are overcomers. Am I now trying to win the approval of man or of God? If I were still trying to please people, I would not be a servant of Christ. My friends, I do not feel that I have already arrived. I run toward the goal so that I can win the prize of being called to heaven. (Galatians 1:10 AMP, Philippians 3:13-14 GNT).

A heterosexual person can go to hell too. Romans 8:9 says that *without the Spirit of Christ, you do not belong to Christ.* Those who are not filled with the Holy Spirit must seek to be empowered themselves. According to Acts 1:8, speaking in tongues is the power to be a witness. The 'church' must recognize that homosexuality means a person who is sexually attracted to people of their own sex. What I mean by this is they are human beings toiling with "unnatural lust." You don't have to be afraid to approach them. Be led by the Spirit of God.

Some gay people need to hear about the love of God, and others need to know that hell does exist. The homosexual spirit can be so bold that believers must be wise in their approach. Do not give gay people your opinion and 'preach at them.' You might mean well, but it causes people's flesh to rebel because the devil does not want to set them free anyway. *For the sinful nature is always hostile to God. It never did obey God's laws, and it never will* (Romans 8:7 NLT). You will be more effective ministering to the LGBTQ community when you draw them with lovingkindness. When God instructs you to do something, it will always be effective. Otherwise, pray because that is a weapon in itself.

For twenty years, I searched for fulfillment. I regret ever getting tattoos with names that I have no idea where the people are today. After childhood sexual abuse, abandonment issues, rejection, church hurt, gender confusion, perversion, gunfire, gang affiliation, drug addiction, alcoholism, promiscuity, car wrecks, domestic violence, overdosing, alcohol poisoning, public humiliation, and assault with a deadly object; I AM STILL STANDING BY THE GRACE OF GOD.

I should have been dead, but I am a walking testimony. I could not die. I had to live to tell my story. Regardless of my track record, God hired me anyway. *"Choosing rather to suffer affliction with the people of God, than to enjoy the pleasures of sin for a season"* (Hebrews 11:25 KJV). Honestly, I had some fun moments, but there were times that I was tormented.

HOMOSEXUALITY IS A MANIFESTATION OF SOMETHING DEEPER.

Behind every story is a story. A lot of things that I did were a result of intoxication. Addiction was a hiding place to escape from the reality of my unproductive life, and avoid emotional wounds. Yet, I still could not cover every single encounter in this book, but my goal was to disclose enough to help someone else get saved and delivered. My life has truly changed for the better.

I was assigned this mountain to encourage others it can be moved.

You know you have reached a level of maturity when you can pray for your enemies. Enduring years of bondage, I am learning that true freedom is found under the protective authority of the Lord. I have been transformed to testify of the mercies of God, His unfailing love, redeeming power, and goodness toward me. I have been chosen to witness to a generation of lost souls.

This process was like the metamorphosis of a "Caterpillar to Butterfly."

I am so grateful to God for my mother interceding on my behalf. Mother is a prayer warrior who waged warfare in the Spirit. Even when it seemed like the harder she prayed the worse I got, she still believed God. I cannot tell you the countless times that I came home drunk and high, and she undressed me rubbing anointed oil all over my body.

"Satan, I command you to loose your hold. Let my baby go in the name of Jesus," Mom said. She treated all my gay friends with love and told them about Jesus. I do not think I would have made it out alive without my mom remaining by my side.

Many suffer from rejection, molestation, and low self-esteem. The largest study ever conducted by Northshore Research Institute proved the theory of "gay genes" to be FALSE. The devil attacks many children at an early age with same sex attraction because they are too young to fight it. When a child or teenager has been sexually violated by the same sex, the sensation they experienced can confuse them into assuming that they are gay because of the stimulation of their hormones. On the other hand, if one is taken advantage of by the opposite sex it can cause them to turn away from being heterosexual. Pornography and masturbation are other avenues that open the door to the spirit of homosexuality. Masturbation is an act of engaging in sex with a spirit, which is the same sex – "yourself." Pornographic images cause "fantasy" to infiltrate the thought process triggering perversion.

It is the enemy's agenda to kill off the man because he carries the seed.

Procreation is the order of God.

The spirit of homosexuality is trending because Daniel 11:37 states that the antichrist will not desire a woman. Lucifer was kicked out of heaven for saying he will be like the Most High God. Since he oversaw the music in heaven, his two largest platforms today are music and homosexuality. Music was designed to worship God, and populating the Earth was a command in Genesis.

The devil has hijacked the rainbow. The Bible says, *"I have set my rainbow in the clouds, and it will be the sign of the covenant between me and the earth"* (Genesis 9:13 NIV). God is not pleased with this rebellious spirit in the land. I lived on that dark path, and now I am who God unmistakably made me to be. I will not live blinded in deception any longer.

THE DEVIL HAS DONE SUCH A GOOD JOB CAMOUFLAGING THE LIFESTYLE BY CALLING IT "ACCEPTANCE."

People don't even realize we are fighting for lives. We are losing casualties of war every day when a child has gender identity issues. It is a spirit like any other sin. We are suffering more losses to this war than we are in Afghanistan.

Our nation's Constitution was based on biblical principles. The government has passed LGBTQ laws as if this is a race. The Bible is our moral compass. A person must totally disregard the teaching of the Bible to live a homosexual lifestyle. Perversion is against God, nature, and your own body. The imminent return of the Lord is at the door. Many are deceived into believing a sinful lifestyle will get them into heaven.

Sexual orientation is a choice.

Don't you realize that those who do wrong will not inherit the kingdom of God? Don't fool yourselves. Those who indulge in sexual sin, who worship idols, commit adultery, are male prostitutes, practice homosexuality, are thieves, greedy people, drunkards, are abusive or cheat people – none of these will inherit the kingdom of God. Do not conform to the pattern of this world but be transformed by the renewing of your mind. 1 Corinthians 6:9-10 NLT, Romans 12:2a (NIV)

I want to encourage anyone living in sin to obey the plan of salvation. *"Repent, and be baptized every one of you in the name of Jesus Christ for the remission of sins, and ye shall receive the gift of the Holy Ghost,"* (Acts 2:38 KJV). Repentance is a remorseful change of mind. Baptism in the name of JESUS is a command of God (Mark 16:16) to wash away your sins. The Holy Ghost with the evidence of speaking in tongues (Acts 2:4) is the power to live holy. This constitutes the new birth (John 3:5).

That worldly walk of foolishness leads you nowhere. Sin took me farther than I wanted to go, kept me longer than I wanted to stay, and cost me more than I wanted to pay. I made so many wrong turns, but through God's loving mercy, I still ended up in the right place. He made my detour a turn around. I encourage you to comply with God's standards and let your path be straight. *One thing I ask from the Lord, this only do I seek: that I may dwell in the house of the Lord all the days of my life* (Psalm 27:4 NIV).

I am the "NEW LGBT," which means LOVER OF GOD, BELIEVER OF TRUTH. What took twenty minutes to get into, has taken twenty years to come out of. Be careful what you try once because you might become addicted. Jesus died to eradicate our sins. "I was born to be a backbone." Thank you Jesus I escaped from "Behind Enemy Lines," and you can too!

Nichol Collins

Be transformed ...

Transformation

... by the renewing of your mind. (Rom. 12:2)

Nichol Collins

Pastor & Lady Gentry Richardson Bethlehem Temple

237

The race must be ran until the end !

"Peter replied, 'Each one of you must repent of your sins and turn to God, and be baptized in the name of JESUS Christ for the forgiveness of your sins. Then you will receive the gift of the Holy Spirit.'"
Acts 2:38 (NLT)

"Jesus replied, 'I assure you, no one can enter the Kingdom of God without being born of water and the Spirit.'"
John 3:5 (NLT)

"When you follow the desires of your sinful nature, the results are very clear: sexual immorality, impurity, lustful pleasures, idolatry, sorcery, hostility, quarreling, jealousy, outbursts of anger, selfish ambition, dissension, division, envy, drunkenness, wild parties, and other sins like these. Let me tell you again, as I have before, that anyone living that sort of life will not inherit the Kingdom of God."
Galatians 5:19-21 (NLT)

"So God created human beings in his own image. In the image of God he created them; male and female he created them." Genesis 1:27 (NLT)

"I have set my rainbow in the clouds, and it will be the sign of the covenant between me and the earth."
Genesis 9:13 (NIV)

"Do not practice homosexuality, having sex with another man as with a woman. It is a detestable sin."
Leviticus 18:22 (NLT)

"A woman must not put on men's clothing, and a man must not wear women's clothing. Anyone who does this is detestable in the sight of the LORD your God."
Deuteronomy 22:5 (NLT)

"Or do you not know that the unrighteous will not inherit the kingdom of God? Do not be deceived; neither fornicators, nor idolaters, nor adulterers, nor effeminate, nor homosexuals, nor thieves, nor the covetous, nor drunkards, nor revilers, nor swindlers, will inherit the kingdom of God"
1 Corinthians 6:9-10 (NASB)

"That is why God abandoned them to their shameful desires. Even the women turned against the natural way to have sex and instead indulged in sex with each other. And the men, instead of having normal sexual relations with women, burned with lust for each other. Men did shameful things with other men, and as a result of this sin, they suffered within themselves the penalty they deserved. Since they thought it foolish to acknowledge God, he abandoned them to their foolish thinking and let them do things that should never be done. Their lives became full of every kind of wickedness, sin, greed, hate, envy, murder, quarreling, deception, malicious behavior, and gossip. They are backstabbers, haters of God, insolent, proud, and boastful. They invent new ways of sinning, and they disobey their parents. They refuse to understand, break their promises, are heartless, and have no mercy. They know God's justice requires that those who do these things deserve to die, yet they do them anyway. Worse yet, they encourage others to do them, too"
Romans 1:26-32 (NLT)

Made in the USA
Monee, IL
02 March 2024

54330693R00148